If you would like an extra wedding invitation, write Dr. Gallatin. The address is on page 282.

Wedding Invitation

Dr. Gallatin, Thanks for everything.

My Fiancé _____ and I would like to invite you to our wedding.

_____
day   month   year

_____
place

(   ) _____
phone   signature

Please Print

Name _____

Address _____

City _____

State _____ Zip ____

Dr. Martin V. Gallatin
80 East 11th Street, Suite 440
New York, NY 10003

How To
GET
MARRIED
In a Year or Less

By
Martin V. Gallatin, Ph.D.

S.p.i.
BOOKS

S.P.I. BOOKS

A division of Shapolsky Publishers, Inc.

For any additional information, contact:

S.P.I. BOOKS
136 West 22nd Street, New York, NY 10011

Tel. (212) 633-2022
Fax (212) 633-2123

ISBN 1-56171-062-8

First Edition 1987

1 2 3 4 5 6 7 8 9 10

Typography by Smith, Inc., New York

Manufactured in the United States of America

Affirmation

I, _____ _____ , have
made up my mind to meet and marry the kind of person
I want in a year or even less. I know love is just a hello
away. I will not settle for someone who is just OK. I don't
have to. I will not allow temporary disappointments
to slow me down. I will do everything in my power to
attract and date someone special and then develop a
fulfilling relationship. I will make no excuses for my past
actions, and expect to be in a loving relationship shortly.
I will take advantage of every social opportunity.

I will make sufficient time for my social life. I realize
there is no right place or right way to meet my partner.
There is no shortage of people I could date regardless of
my age and present circumstances. I want the pleasure,
happiness, and security a good marriage provides. I will
send Dr. Gallatin the enclosed wedding invitation when
I become engaged.

PERMISSIONS

Drawings pp. 22, 23, 43, 57, 60, 77, 96, 109, 146, 147, 155, 171, 192, 209, 216, 229. Reprinted from Kiss Me You Fool by Andrew Vines; Copyright © 1984 by Andrew Vines. Used by permission of Clarkson N. Potter, Inc.

"I met my first husband at Bloomingdale's and my second husband at "Banana Republic." Drawing by Dana Fradon, p. 100; © 1986 The New Yorker Magazine, Inc.

Captionless. Cowboy's landscape saying. Drawing by Mort Gerberg, p. 143; © 1982 Don't Bother, Forget It, Hopeless...The New Yorker Magazine, Inc. Maybe Maybe Maybe Maybe...The New Yorker Magazine, Inc.

"Hi. I need no introduction. Who are you?" Drawing by Mort Gerberg, p. 5; © 1977 The New Yorker Magazine, Inc.

"Memory of Various Women." Drawing by W. Steig, p. 245; © 1977 The New Yorker Magazine, Inc.

"Young, rich, and restless." Drawing by Dedini, p. 181; © 1986. "That's a career?" The New Yorker Magazine, Inc.

"Like Shirley MacLaine, Doris is fifty and has great legs." Drawing by Lorenz, p. 196; © 1984 The New Yorker Magazine, Inc.

"We're in love." "Details at Eleven." Drawing by Mankoff, p. 175; © 1986 The New Yorker Magazine, Inc.

"And the man on her right is Dr. Martin Gallatin." Drawing by Li-mor Raviv, p. 252.

Drawings pp. 49, 116, 130, 162 © Maine Line Company, Rockport, Maine.

Drawings pp. 66, 157 © Nicole Hollander. Published by Maine Line Company, Rockport, Maine.

"Love on the R Train," by Deirdre Carmody, Oct. 25, 1986, p. 107; and "Chance Meeting Ends, Seaman's Search Begins," Drawing by Susan Heller Anderson and David W. Dunlap, of Aug. 11, 1986, p. 10; © 1986 by The New York Times Company. Reprinted by permission.

Acknowledgments

How to Get Married in a Year or Less is dedicated to my mother Zelda, my brother Jeffrey, Jack Sheck, Richard Smith, Barry Cohen, Steve Malkin and Janet Feder.

I want to thank the thousands of people who have attended my lectures, seminars, and programs since 1978. Your questions, suggestions, and encouragement have made this book what it is. I look forward to hearing of your social success.

Many thanks to my editor, Isaac Mozeson, whose devotion and skills are everywhere present.

Preface

Dear Reader:

The only purpose of *How to Get Married in a Year or Less* is to comfortably get you down the aisle of romance, love and marriage as fast as possible. The book is for singles who have decided they no longer want to be single or are fed up with being single. *How to Get Married in a Year or Less* will show how you can attract your first choice for a mate regardless of how poor your statistical prospects appear to be.

Pay no attention to anyone (even your own mother) who tells you you will not be able to find a mate. You only need one good one, and that person is near you right now.

While everyone would like to be introduced to their mate by a family member or a friend—this doesn't always happen. There is no right place or right way to meet your partner. This book will teach you how to meet your partner wherever you are, without changing your personality. Supermarkets, libraries and museums offer many overlooked possibilities for finding love in the course of your everyday life. Bars, social activities and personal ads can provide further opportunities to meet your life partner.

The ideas, advice, and techniques presented in this book have changed the lives of many people, and I have the wedding invitations and letters to prove it.

Best Wishes,
Martin
New York, January 1992

Chapter Titles

1. Your Single Days Are Numbered
2. Going Out
3. What You Want
4. Meeting. . .Wherever You Are
5. Dating for Marriage
6. The Available You
7. It Begins With Hello
8. Beating Rejection
9. Enjoying Safe Sex When You Are Ready
10. Loving a Busy Professional
11. You Still Have Time
12. Single Parents: New Loves And Families

Congratulations

Contents

Affirmation iii
Acknowledgments v
Preface vii

Chapter 1
Your Single Days Are Numbered 1
Getting Started 2
You Don't Need More Than a Year 3
Every Moment Is a Single's Event 4
Ways to Meet 6
A Better Social Life 6
Picking Your Man 7
More Opportunities to Meet Than Ever 7
The Difficulties in Finding a Good Partner 8
Being Single Is No Crime 9
Social Success 11
Seminars on "How to Meet" or "How to Flirt" 11
Conventional Wisdom and Your Quest for Love 12
Too Busy to Get Married 15
Let's Step Out 15

Chapter 2
Going Out 17
Getting Started 18
Confidently Single 19
Why Singles Detest Singles Events 19
A Word to the Wise 20
Advantages of the Singles Scene 20
Disadvantages of the Singles Scene 21

Contents

Stay Tuned 21
One is All You Need 21
Your Best Shot 21
Don't Join An Organization 24
The Six Excuses 24
Warning 26
Questions to Ask Before Attending
Singles Events or Clubs 26
Questions to Ask Before Joining a Dating Service 27
Singles Activities to Attend 27
Check Please 27
Fewer Opportunities 28
The Singles Scene 28
Activity Review 42
Don't Forget The Bars 44
Beating Bar Bias 44
Exploding Singles Bars Myths 44
The Bars In Town 46
Who You Will Meet 48
You Need a Good Attitude 49
When To Go 50
Gentlemen 50
Ladies 50
Navigating the Bar 51

Chapter 3

What You Want 53

Getting Started 54
Your Love Priorities 55
Love Is Not a Battlefield 56
Don't Get Stuck 57

Contents

Seeing Yourself and Others 58
Who You Want 59
No One Around 59
Never Satisfied 60
The Passive Trap 60
Why Women Hesitate to Ask Men 61
Getting Her Man 62
Why Men Don't Approach 62
Your Ideal Marriage Partner 63
My Marriage Partner 64
Expect to Do Well 65
Don't Get Sidetracked 67
Current Social Goals 67
Let's Get Emotional 67
Time for Love 68
Holding the Hands of Time 68
Lover Profile 69

Chapter 4

Meeting. . .Wherever You Are 71
Meeting Naturally 72
Roadblocks to Meeting Anywhere 74
It's Mother Nature's Way 76
Where to Meet 76
Dr. Gallatin's Top Ten Ways to Meet a Mate 77
Be Chosen 80
Dr. Gallatin's Eight Steps to Be Married
in a Year or Less 80
Dr. Gallatin's Tips for Meeting Anyone,
Anywhere, Anytime 87
Dr. Gallatin's Tips 87

Keep These in Mind 98
Lover Shopping at Bloomingdale's 101

Chapter 5

The Available You 103

On The Shelf 104
The Real You 104
Getting Flustered 105
On the Tip of Your Tongue 105
What You Have to Offer 108
Use Your Strengths 108
What's Missing? 109
Gaining Favorable Attention 112
Body Language 115
Are You Flirting Enough? 117
Women Need to Flirt 117
How to Get a Fix on Someone 118

Chapter 6

It Begins With Hello. . . 119

Getting It Going 120
The Moment of Truth 121
Your Attitude 121
How to Ask Him Comfortably 121
What's a Person Like You Doing
With a Line Like This? 123
Purposeful Listening 123
Getting Past the Opener 124
Opening Up 124
Starters 127
Excuse Me 127

Contents

Getting Unstuck 128
The Six Steps of a Conversation 129
Yes, I Can't 135
Pest Control 136
A "No" Need Not End a Conversation 137
An Example of Not Saying "No" 137
Ralph, How About Friday Night? 137
Why Men Don't Ask 138

Chapter 7

Beating Rejection 139

Reject Rejection 140
"Who's Next" 140
You Haven't Been Totally Rejected 141
Don't Be Beaten Before You Start 141
Home Run Hitters Strike Out Most 141
Consequences of the Fear of Rejection 142
Rejection's Family Ties 144
Total Acceptance 144
All Rejection Is Not the Same 145
Personal Rejection 145
Circumstantial Rejection 145
You May Need More Rejection 146
Sooner Is Better Than Later 147
Immediate Rejection 148
Rejection After a Few Dates 148
Rejection After Sex 149
Rejection After You Become Involved 150
You Have to Be Accepted Before
You Can Be Rejected 150
Reducing Your Chances of Being Rejected 151
Rejected Again 151

Contents

Chapter 8
**Enjoying Safe Sex
When You Are Ready 153**
The Sex Factor 154
Sexual Compatability 155
Sexual Compatability Isn't Love 156
79 Positions 156
Handling Advances 157
The One-Night Stand 158
Do You Need Your Doorman's
or Neighbor's Approval? 158
Should You or Shouldn't You? 159
Love and Sex 160
Saying "No" With Your Foot in the Door 160
I Don't Usually, But. . . 161
What Turns Women On 163
If Your Body Is Not Perfect 163
If He Doesn't Act, You Can 164
Love or Obligation? 165

Chapter 9
Loving a Busy Professional 167
Getting Started 168
Fitting Love In 169
No Time for Love 169
Too Much Time for Love 170
People Professions 170
Business Success Alone Won't Get You Married 170
The Best Jobs for Meeting Mates 171
Executive Sweet 172

Contents

Get There First 173

Mixing Business With Pleasure 173

From Business to Pleasure 174

Love in the Supply Room 176

Advantages of Meeting in the Workplace 177

Can You Handle an Office Romance? 177

When an Office Romance Goes Sour 178

Working Women 178

All Businesses Are Not The Same 178

Having Lunch 179

Lingering After Five 180

People Meet and Date at Work Every Day 180

Marrying Money 181

Don't Make Excuses 182

Too Much to Offer 183

What Do You Do for a Living? 183

Are You a Female Businessman or
a Woman in Business? 184

Talking to the Professional Man 184

What Professional Men Want 185

You Have Not Waited Too Long 186

Dating a Busy Professional 186

Chapter 10

You Still Have Time 189

Getting Started 190

It's Never Too Late to Say "Yes" 191

Beware of the "Lonatic" 191

Getting Out There Right Now 192

Divorced but Not Free 193

On the Road Again 193

Contents

Putting It Behind You 194
The Widow's Plight 195
Preparing Yourself for Reality 195
The Good News 197
Advantages of Being Over Forty 197
Thirty-Nine Plus 198
Dating Again 199
Middle Age Dating 199
Exploding the Myths About Middle Age Dating 200
A Younger Man! 201
Why Women Don't Date Younger Men 202
Winning Over a Confirmed Bachelor 203
Married Too Many Times? 203

Chapter 11

Dating For Marriage 205

Getting Started 206
Dating Without Unnecessary Games 208
Dating Should Be Fun 210
Do's and Don'ts of the First Three Dates 210
End It at Date Two if the Person Is Not for You 210
The First Three Dates 212
The First Call 213
Closing the Call 214
Before Your First Date 215
First Time Out 215
What Do We Do? 217
Two on the Town 218
Afterwards 218
Between Dates 219

Ending a Date Early 219
Date Two 220
End It at Date Two If the Person Is Not for You 221
Date Three 221
Dr. Gallatin's Eight Steps to Know if Someone
is a Serious Possibility 222
Benefits of the Eight Steps 224
Dating More Than One Person at a Time 224
Building a Lasting Relationship 224
Dr. Gallatin's Pointers for Developing
a Lifetime Relationship 225
How to Get Over a Plateau 226
Types of Intimacy 226
Getting Serious 227
Reaching a Commitment 227
Allergic to Marriage 228
Right on Schedule 228
Living Together 228
Dr. Gallatin's Guidelines for Living Together 230
Have a State of the Union Meeting 230
Do You Need a Private Eye? 231
Prenuptial Agreements 231
How to Get Him to the Alter 232
How to Get Her to the Alter 233

Chapter 12

Single Parents: New Loves And Families 235

Make Time for Love 236
A Year Is Enough 237
Not Again 237

Contents

Digging Up Bones 238
Single and a Mother 238
Single Dads 239
Too Busy for Love 240
Back in Circulation 240
Dr. Gallatin's Seven Tips for Single Parents 241
You Have No Competition 246
Your Love Choices 246
Squeezing Sex In 247
Never Married, but a Parent 247
Not Your Children 248

Congratulations 249

On Your Way 250
Invite Me to Your Wedding 251

Has Your Group, Organization or Business
Heard Dr. Gallatin Yet? 253
Hear Dr. Gallatin on Audiotape 255
Free Tape Offer 256

1

Your Single Days
Are Numbered

"You only need one
good one, and that
person is near you
right now."

— Dr. Gallatin

Getting Started

*L**ove is just a hello away.* I am warning you, if you continue reading this book you will be married in a year or even less. You don't always have to be the first to say hello, but you do have to use every social opportunity that presents itself. You either have to let someone meet you, or you have to go out and meet him or her. Regardless of who you are, where you live, how you were raised, how much money you have, how old you are, how outgoing, what problems you have or think you have, you can be happily married—in a year or less.

Meeting the right person has become a preoccupation in one way or another for the millions of American singles searching for love and marriage.

How to Get Married in a Year or Less presents the answer to the basic concerns of singles, which are:

- Locating the right men and women.
- Meeting the best person in the most natural way.
- Developing a relationship.
- Marrying the best person with the confidence that the marriage will be happy and lasting.

Just getting married is not good enough. Since 1980, 497 out of every 1,000 marriages have ended in the divorce courts, according to Dr. Lenore J. Weitzman in her book *The Divorce Revolution*. She further reveals that almost forty percent of these divorces occur within four years of the wedding.

A recent U.S. Census Bureau report stated that six out of ten women in their thirties will get divorced.

Just looking at the statistics can be devastating. In an analysis of information drawn from census data, three Yale sociologists—Dr. Neil Bennett, Dr. David E. Bloom, and Patricia H. Craig—concluded, in part, that "college-educated white women who have not married by the time they are twenty-five years old have only a fifty percent chance of marrying." If you didn't go to college your chances are slightly better, and if you are a black woman they become slightly worse. When you reach age thirty, the odds go down to twenty percent and at age thirty-five they drop to five percent. At age forty, the number is perhaps one percent. These conclusions were based on a study of 70,000 households.

After the release of these shocking statistics, panic set in and women became more discouraged than ever. Cover stories appeared in *People* and *Newsweek*, among others, and the authors were invited to television and radio shows to explain their findings.

While the statistics were put under a microscope, the analysis was largely neglected. In an interview published in the *New York Times*, Dr. Bloom said: "Our study is a study of aggregate behavior. It is not a study of individuals. We are not taking into account the most important things about individual people getting married, things like whether or not they want to." The statistics speak for themselves. Finding a good mate in today's society is not easy.

You Don't Need More Than a Year

After talking to thousands of people since 1978, I have discovered that the average meet-to-marriage sequence takes no more than a year. You may not actually tie the knot in the year because you need to save money or finish school first. The fact that you are not formally married is only a technicality—you are a committed couple who will be married soon. Younger or less experienced people may need somewhat more time. For someone who is experienced and knows what he or she wants, a year may be a long time.

It only takes three months of regular dating or so to get to know someone well. After a certain point it is "go" or "no go." Dragging the courtship out doesn't mean you will learn any significant new information or increase your chances of getting married and staying married. A deadline helps to guide you and to put things in perspective.

Every Moment Is a Single's Event

You shouldn't have to go out of your way to meet a mate. In the course of your everyday personal and business life, you see any number of people who are attractive and available. Many of these potential candidates would be glad to talk with you. Several of them would go out with you, and at least one (who is good for you) would want to develop a relationship and get married. You only need to meet one right person. Unfortunately, we have not been encouraged to look for or to take advantage of social opportunities when we are out shopping, at the library, having lunch or taking a stroll. Most people I have interviewed said that while out shopping they are thinking only of their food shopping list.

How to Get Married in a Year or Less will show you how to minimize the possibility of personal rejection and public humiliation, while at the same time encouraging you to take advantage of every social opportunity that comes along—wherever you happen to be.

Of course, meeting naturally wherever you are means talking to strangers. A stranger is merely someone whom you have yet to meet. While it is understandable that you are reluctant to talk to strangers, the fact is that strangers are more apt to be boring than treacherous. When you meet an attractive, available stranger you have an opportunity to get to know this person.

"Hi. I need no introduction. Who are you?"

Drawing by Mort Gerberg: © 1977 The New Yorker Magazine, Inc.

Ways to Meet

❦ By personal introduction.
❦ By attending singles activities.
❦ Wherever you are.

Most of us don't get introduced often enough to people we are really interested in. The commercial singles scene is continually disappointing. Meeting people wherever you are allows you to choose who you want, when you want, and have a steady flow of new possibilities.

No matter which of the three methods of meeting you happen to be using at a particular time, you will have to apply similar techniques to win the person over.

Meeting someone requires you to approach a person in a way that makes you approachable—to begin the conversation or to maintain it, to ask the person out or to know how to encourage an offer for a future contact.

A Better Social Life

I assume that the reader has a social life but wants to speed up the process of finding an appropriate mate. While you may not have any special difficulty that prevents you from having a meaningful social life, everyone has an area that he or she could improve. For some, it is the initial approach; for others, it is enhancing their conversational skills; and for still others, it is turning a date into a relationship. Which area would you like to do better in?

Picking Your Man

Today's women are surrounded by single men in the workplace. Yet many women are not meeting enough good men. Even a busy calendar doesn't mean you have a satisfying social life. The man you are seeing may not be the one who you want to be the father of your children—as good as his sense of humor may be.

With the fierce competition for the best men, women have to make the most of every situation. This might even mean being outrageous and asking a man for his opinion about a pair of sunglasses while at a department store.

Take the example of Ruth. After attending a *How to Get Married in a Year or Less* seminar in Manhattan, she caught the Second Avenue bus, sat down and spotted a man she found attractive. Contrary to her usual behavior, she didn't passively look away. She smiled directly at him. He returned her smile, and before she knew what happened he was sitting next to her, introducing himself. Before she reached her destination, they'd made a date to get together the following Thursday at the Metropolitan Museum of Art. It isn't always this easy, but sometimes it can be.

More Opportunities to Meet Than Ever

Today we have more opportunities to meet potential mates than ever before. You don't have to wait for love. We are not restricted to the church, family and our neighborhood. The world has gotten smaller and we can meet more people in more places in a more relaxed way.

There have never been more singles of every age seeking marriage. Yet many singles are left on their own, as the family, the church, and neighborhood institutions provide fewer leads. You will not be on your own if you use the advice in this book.

The traditional view of how a gentleman can meet a lady is expressed by Emily Post who says he, "may not use a lunch counter, bus or retrieved glove as the basis for an introduction; the traditionally correct introduction, made by a mutual friend, is still necessary." A gentleman today has more opportunities to make his interest known. A woman, when asked, can give her name and number if she feels the groundwork has been tastefully laid. Today, women have many more chances to select their marriage partner discretely. After reading this book you will be able to meet who you want, when you want, where you want. The eight steps offered will show you how. It will be our secret.

The Difficulties in Finding a Good Partner

While walking down Chicago's Michigan Avenue, I overheard two women talking about men. One said to the other, "It is so arduous," and the other replied, "It's already too late." What struck me was that both women were articulate, attractive, and only in their mid-to-late twenties.

These women feel frustrated, discouraged, and drained because seeking a mate involves the following:

❦ Continually attempting to meet new people.
❦ Searching for new places to go out, hoping your luck will improve.

❧ Always presenting yourself in the most positive light.

❧ Becoming emotionally involved—often unexpectedly.

❧ Subjecting yourself to the possibility of immediate or eventual rejection.

❧ Not knowing how to act on the first few dates because the rules are not as straightforward as they used to be.

Being Single Is No Crime

Anyone who has been single for a number of years can tell you that it is harder to meet the right person today. Singles have become increasingly cynical. They often don't really make the effort or believe enough in themselves.

Many people who have been single too long are just plain worn out, and are suffering from romantic battle fatigue. The more they go out the more disappointed they are. Just when things seem to be going well, something happens and the relationship comes to a sudden halt.

Many singles are very wrapped up with themselves, and don't give viable marriage prospects a real chance. It can be very discouraging to keep running into such people, who seem like good potential mates but are ultimately not marriage material.

Finding a mate today is too often a business trans-action rather than a merging of chemistry, romance, shared values and the desire for unconditional love. Many a man or woman who wants emotional security is settling, instead, for financial security. Rather than giving the financially well-off an advantage, this situation makes it all the harder for him or her to attract a sincerely loving mate.

Being single today is perfectly acceptable, regardless of one's age. Many people in their thirties, forties and older are single.

The *U.S. News and World Report* stated that four out of every hundred couples are unmarried and living together. In many cases, singles are unmarried but not alone.

One no longer has to make an excuse for being single, but this doesn't make it any more desirable. My interviews clearly show that if the average single finds the mate that she or he wants, arrangements for the wedding would be under way. Lack of desire to get married is a result of having no one in your life you really want to marry.

Chance Meeting Ends, Seaman's Search Begins

"**H**er name was Nancy — that's it, Nancy. I didn't even get her last name."

Countless tales of heartbreak followed the sailors on liberty during Liberty Weekend as surely and fleetingly as the wakes of their ships.

But Journalist Seaman Greg White of the U.S.S. Dahlgren, a guided-missile destroyer, shared his heartbreak in a letter to this newspaper:

"She is a beautiful brunette of 27 years who stands 4 feet, 11 inches tall. I know that must narrow it down to a mere 14,284 people. I also know that she works in a paint store during the day and studies interior design at night. She lives in Manhattan. O.K., here's the clincher: she has a sailor hat with the Social Security number 023-60-7887 in it.

"I guess it's pretty obvious the effect this woman had on me. In the five and a half hours we talked, I learned a little about people and a lot about myself. I think one of the worst things in the world is to make a friend and be condemned to the fact that you will never see him/her again."

Deven Black manages the North Star Pub at 93 South Street, where the two met on July 5. "That's a tough one," he said, trying to conjure this Nancy. "Her name doesn't ring a bell. Four-foot-11 doesn't. Nothing about her connects with any of our regulars."

But the North Star sounds like a good place for budding romance. Mr. Black points out that four of his bartenders who started work as bachelors are now married. Two regular patrons who met at the pub were married last month. They will be treated to a free anniversary dinner, he said, "for the rest of their lives — or as long as we last."

Will Seaman White find Nancy? "Well, I'm optimistic," the sailor wrote. "I believe, in this day of renewed patriotism, romance also has a chance."

Susan Heller Anderson
David W. Dunlap

It is one thing not to be married; it is another not to regularly have good relationships with marriageable candidates. One doesn't want a reputation for avoiding serious involvements.

It is acceptable to be single today. Not so many years ago, being single beyond a certain age made you a "spinster" or a "playboy." With so many people not married and with divorce being so prevalent, one's chances of being single again at some point is a reality. No group is immune: even ministers are getting divorced in record numbers.

Social Success

You are a social success when you can talk to anyone, anywhere, anytime and walk away whenever you want without the fear of rejection. Socially successful people only think about meeting someone when they see an individual who attracts them and is their type. You will meet many nice people who don't have these good social skills, even though they are well educated and hold executive positions. While it is easier to meet and have a relationship with a socially competent person, you can find your match even if his social skills are not as good as yours.

Seminars on "How to Meet" or "How to Flirt"

Adult education centers (like the nationwide "Learning Annex"), Y's and colleges are increasingly offering courses, seminars, and workshops for singles. Titles range from "Lover Shopping at Bloomingdale's" to "How to Marry a Much Younger Man."

Some people attend because it is a comfortable way to meet others. They want to brush up on their social savvy. Perhaps they have not been going out regularly or never really developed good social skills and have decided it is still not too late to learn.

Take Morris. He attended a singles workshop because he had a date with a woman half his age and it didn't work out. When questioned, he admitted that even though he was ten minutes late, he stopped to get a cup of coffee to take out. He sipped his coffee while talking with his date, and she somehow refused his offer to go out with him for dinner.

Another man registered for a singles seminar because he had left a religious order to find a wife and start a family. He was thirty-eight and had never learned how to relate to women.

The quality of the instruction varies greatly. Titles are just titles. Read the course descriptions and the instructors' credentials carefully. If both seem in order, why not take a chance? Even if you don't learn that much, you have an opportunity to meet like-minded people.

Conventional Wisdom and Your Quest for Love

Much of what we hold to be true about finding a mate actually prevents us from getting married. The most important conventional wisdom is presented here along with Dr. Gallatin's position. Throughout *How to Get Married in a Year or Less*, you will see how the conventional wisdom may be holding you back.

Conventional Wisdom	**Dr. Gallatin Says**
Only in very special circumstances should a woman approach a man.	Women can make the first move if the man doesn't. The secret is how to do it.
When you look for love, you will never find it.	If you don't look for love, you are unlikely to find it.
Strangers are dangerous, and are to be avoided, unless you are properly introduced.	Strangers are more likely to be boring than dangerous. Your next lover is a stranger today.
There are few quality single men and women available today.	There is only a shortage if you don't know how to meet them.
It is only a matter of time before you will meet someone.	You could wait for years and not find the right person, and then panic and marry almost anyone.
There are special places where good quality prospects go.	There is no right place to meet a mate. It is not where you go that is important, but what you do when you spot someone who interests you— whether it is at a dance or a museum.

Searching for a mate is drudgery.

If you follow Dr. Gallatin's advice, you will have many quality dates and be married within a year.

If you are a woman over forty, you will not find a mate—nor the man you really desire.

It is never too late to get a good man if you want one and know how to find one.

You have to be constantly looking for a mate.

You only need to think about meeting a mate when you see someone who interests you.

You will never find someone you really want.

You will find the best person when you decide that you are ready.

You need to be charismatic, rich, outgoing, or have special characteristics to get the best mate.

You need to be motivated, skilled, and confident.

All you have to do is to meet that right person.

You have to know how to talk, date, develop a relationship and get a commitment.

Rejection is inevitable and to be dreaded.

Rejection does not have to be your constant companion.

You need a good line to get a conversation going.	You need to know how to naturally begin and maintain a conversation.
You cannot meet someone worthwhile at singles events/bars/discos.	You can meet the best person at those places if you know what to do and when to do it.
You are not supposed to meet people on trains, in stores, or on the street.	There is no wrong place to meet anyone.

Too Busy to Get Married

Because of conventional wisdom, many singles have developed a life-style that emphasizes friends (more often than not of the same sex) and finding one special person they are comfortable with to take care of their love/sex needs but who may not be available for marriage.

We get too busy with our careers and with trips to the health club. We are often so busy being single that we don't leave ourselves any time for being with a new person. One woman who came to a Friday night lecture said, "It would take me a week to schedule him."

The key to success is balance. The longer you put off making it possible to get a mate, the more difficult it will be to get yourself back into the swing of things and the greater the obstacles you will encounter.

Let's Step Out

Now get dressed up, step out, and see what opportunities there are for you.

2

❧

Going Out

"When you see the
right person, you are
in the right place."

— Dr. Gallatin

17

Getting Started

Whether you are recently single, new to the area, don't know where to begin, or have not seriously been looking lately, your first step will be to find out what is going on. You will soon be in contact with the commercial and nonprofit singles scene. These organizations sponsor dances, speakers, local trips, world tours, and matchmaking services of every kind.

The main purpose of commercial singles organizations is to make money. The purpose of nonprofit organizations is to provide opportunities to make social contacts. These groups are run by religious organizations, Y's, community associations and concerned individuals. If your funds are limited or if you have an aversion to being treated like a commodity, then look for a nonprofit activity that you are comfortable with.

The commercial singles scene came into existence to take the place of or supplement the traditional ways of meeting—via the family, religious groups, or well-meaning others. It has never lived up to its promise.

The commercial singles scene only attracts singles who decide to participate. The best candidates for marriage rarely attend single events. Those in the middle range of the desirability spectrum—the bulk of the population—attend on occasion but are self-conscious and often not at their best. Those at the bottom tier of desirability generally use the commercial scene as their only or main source of connecting. They are highly dissatisfied, but at least they have this method of meeting people available.

Some commercial singles activities provide better opportunities for meeting quality people than others. If you carefully select those activities that appear to be best for you, you will meet more suitable people.

Singles make up a body of unconnected individuals competing with each other for a limited supply of acceptable candidates. Since singles rarely work together and help each other, the search for a mate could be long, lonely, and horrible.

This chapter will review the types of services available so you can decide which is best based on your current situation, personality, and financial resources.

Remember, you only need to meet one good person.

Confidently Single

One's attitude about being single can be seen in small things. When you go to a movie or a restaurant and someone asks, "How many?" do you look down and mumble, "Just one," or do you look the person right in the eyes and answer, "One please." If you feel like a second-class citizen, you will be treated like one.

Until you feel that it is all right to be single, you will be uncomfortable attending singles activities. The only thing you'll be courting is failure.

When you are out in the singles marketplace, it will be necessary for you to be as natural and casual as possible in order to attract and to win over the best prospects. The more artificial the environment, the more you have to make others comfortable.

Why Singles Detest Singles Events

Singles feel attending a singles event is a necessary evil. It is seen as a sign of personal failure as singles activities attract a high percentage of people with limited social options. The thought of being in the same room with people whom you wouldn't normally associate with may inhibit you from meeting the good people who are there.

Single activities also attract a high proportion of people who will never get married. Many are professional party goers. Some are good looking and fun to talk with as long as the subject of marriage is not broached. Many are seeking a few hours of diversion, but are not looking for or expecting to meet anyone.

Few singles enjoy attending an activity which is limited to singles. They feel uncomfortable because it is too obvious what they are there to do.

A Word to the Wise

Don't depend on any one activity or any particular strategy to yield the results you want. Mix different activities and groups. For example, you can answer a personal ad and attend a lecture during the same week.

Advantages of the Singles Scene

Let us look at what you get by actively seeking contacts in the singles scene:

- You know the participants are single (with occasional exceptions).
- You know the time, date, and exact location.
- You know the cost.
- You know that some of the people may be generally compatible.

Disadvantages of the Singles Scene

Involvement in the singles scene has the following disadvantages:
- The quality of the participants often leaves a lot to be desired.
- Poor management.
- Lack of personal concern.
- High prices (in some instances).
- Lack of stability.
- Poor reputation in the singles community.

Stay Tuned

To discover the many possibilities in the singles scene, buy magazines, newsletters and newspapers marketed for singles. If a suitable publication fits your budget, it may be a good idea to subscribe.

One is All You Need

Even if the crowd doesn't seem that good, don't panic and leave. There are always some desirable people that should be checked out. Pick the one who interests you the most and meet this person. You usually won't be sorry you made the effort.

Your Best Shot

Dress right, put your chin up, get there on time, circulate, talk with at least three good people, get phone numbers of everyone you want to talk with again, and leave when you are ready.

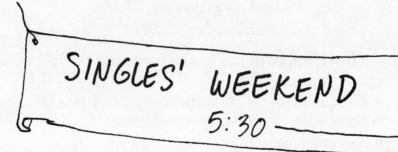

OK, GIRLS. BILL AND I ARE GONNA GET THE FRITOS, THE SANGRIA, AND THE 3-D GLASSES. YOU GO AND GET THE PAPER HATS, THE BLOWERS, AND THE CONTRACEPTIVES, AND WE'LL MEET BACK HERE IN, LET'S SAY, 20 MINUTES.

Don't Join An Organization

If you join a singles organization and meet someone at the first function, or at the video store two days later, you have no reason to attend their upcoming activity. You don't have to be a member of most organizations. Pay the non-member fee for those activities you wish to attend.

You are better off participating in a quality non-membership singles organization like Dick Syatt's dances in the Boston area. Mr. Syatt is the host of the popular "Hotline Radio Dating Show." You can attend one of his seven weekly parties held in different locations, see some familiar faces and plenty of new ones. Pay the nominal entrance fee and just walk up to someone who attracts you and say, "Hi, the music sounds great. Let's dance to this one." You're on your way. *The Boston Globe* says, "The same six words are invariably spoken on the dance floor, at the bar, around the buffet table, even by most of his competitors: 'Dick Syatt runs a nice dance.'"

The Six Excuses

When you participate in organized singles events, you will hear many flimsy excuses why people don't meet.

Since excuses won't get you married, and answers will, the answers for each excuse are provided on the following pages:

Excuse	**Answer**
1. There is nobody here for me.	You only need one good person. Focus on the prospects who interest you. If you begin with your first choice, you will end up doing better than you think.
2. The atmosphere is bad.	It may be. But since you have made the trip, find someone who interests you.
3. The music is too loud.	As soon as you and a good prospect seem to be mutually interested, suggest going to a quiet spot where you will be able to talk casually.
4. It is boring.	When you start talking to a prospect who interests you, you won't be bored by the event.
5. The people are plastic.	Most of the people are only wearing protective plastic coverings. You need only to find one person whose plastic melts with your warmth.

6. The participants have   Many of them will. Look
   a poor attitude.   for the exception and
                              forget the rest.

Don't make excuses, make acquaintances.

WARNING

Too many offers for the singles consumer are investments in futility. Ask all the questions you have. Use the basic questions included here and any others that you want answered. If the answers aren't to your satisfaction, don't waste your time, money, and effort — call another organization.

Questions to Ask Before Attending Singles Events or Clubs

- How long have you been in business?
- What is the ratio of men to women for this type of activity, based on your past experience?
- Do you accept memberships? (If the answer is YES, how many members do you have in total?) How many are active? How many are men? How many are women? What is the charge?
- Do you have a newsletter? How often does it come out? Ask for a sample copy.
- What is the age range of the participants for this type of activity?
- Where does the crowd generally come from?

Questions to Ask Before Joining a Dating Service

❦ How do you do your matching?

❦ What are your qualifications to do this work?

❦ Who does the actual matching?

❦ How long will it take before my first date?

❦ Do you provide events for members to meet?

❦ What are the office hours? Are you open on Saturday? Evenings?

❦ What is the percentage of members with the characteristics you find desirable? For example: age, race, religion, etc.?

Singles Activities to Attend

Only you can make this decision. Look over all the possible choices; then decide, based on your mood, recent experiences, and the degree of effort you want to exert. If you are in doubt or if you are particularly interested in meeting someone special, go to the activity with the greatest probability of success—even if it is not your favorite place.

The best time to join a new group is during its first few events because the management will go all out to ensure success. Singles quickly tire of a place or an organization and are in a perpetual search for new places and new faces. More and better prospects come at the beginning.

Check Please

Many singles resent paying money to meet people. If you are overcharged, you have a right to be angry. If you don't meet someone you like at a particular event, you have a right to be disappointed. No one but yourself can ensure that you'll have a good time. Spending four dollars for a boring talk where there are few prospective mates is no bargain, even if you can stuff yourself with bagels and cream cheese. You might be better off spending twelve dollars going to a nice place and having only a few finger danishes. On the other hand, paying forty-five dollars for an elegant cocktail party doesn't mean you are getting the best value for your money either. It is usually wiser to attend less expensive, prearranged, well-planned events than to hope for elusive romance at the more "exclusive" social events where people are more likely to wander about aimlessly without meeting anyone.

Fewer Opportunities

The number and quality of commercial singles activities have not improved over the past several years because of increased costs, subsequent price resistance, increased fear of sexual diseases, and general dissatisfaction with the outcome. To be successful you have to spend considerable time and money on quality events, not on a quantity of single events.

New ways for singles to meet come and go. We shall concentrate on the means that have stood the test of time and are the most widely available.

The Singles Scene

Computer Dating
Video Dating
Singles Social Clubs

Personal Matchmakers
Singles Weekends
Cruises
Special Interest Groups
Mail Order Love
Rap Groups
Support Groups
Getting Personal
Touch Tones
Dining Clubs

Computer Dating

Do you want a date with your dream-person in the next few weeks? No problem. Just fill out the questionnaire of any one of the numerous computer dating services, enclose it along with your check, and drop it in the nearest letter box. Your list of prospects will arrive in a plain envelope to your postal box or home.

Sounds easy and painless—right? While being matched by computers may strike you as being unromantic, anything that brings two people together is wonderful. Does the impersonal nature of computer dating offer any advantages? One service described itself as "An honest and sincere service to people who would rather not look in public places for suitable companions."

Let's look at the process from beginning to end. The first step is obtaining an application and filling it out. This it where the trouble begins. Most applicants don't fill out the forms honestly. Some people don't know themselves well, and they believe themselves to be better looking than they really are. Others know they are average-looking, but will check "attractive" in hopes of dating more attractive persons who may like them. Applicants tend to err in their favor in order to attract a more desirable prospect.

Questionnaires, no matter how well researched and written, have their limitations. For example, you could check off intelligent (you have an M.B.A.), blond hair, slim, and a good job, but your nervous twitch will not be discovered until you meet your match. Questionnaires don't ask if you have socially undesirable traits. If questions of this type were asked, the pool of possible clients would shrink to such a small number that most services would go out of business. While a service may ask your height and weight, it doesn't always ask how tall you want your partner to be. A tall man may prefer a short woman.

How is the matching actually done? If there are forty-five questions and a number of options to choose from for each question, selection becomes a complex process. The larger the pool you draw from, the more variables you can use.

The quality of the matchmaking is based on the honesty of the applicants, the integrity of the service, and the pool of applicants that the company has to draw on. The major variables that are actually matched up are age, religion, race, education, and geographical location. All the other questions serve the purpose of making you feel like every facet is being considered in the matching process. What happens in reality is that if you prefer a date from Los Angeles, and there is no one who fits the five other major variables, you will be given the name of someone from San Diego rather than be put on hold or given a refund. When you join, the service has to supply you with names and numbers in short order or give you your money back. Do you know anyone who has gotten a refund? Computer matching provides you with a blind date—with all its liabilities.

The principal users of computer dating services are those who are socially inexperienced or who feel they have too many limitations to compete in the open market. For those who cannot easily get dates, the computer will at least give them an opportunity. But this type of service is not generally recommended as a means of meeting one's ideal mate.

Video Dating

If computer dating doesn't appeal to you, what about video dating? This approach allows members to see each of the other members on tape and then decide who they would like to meet. Sounds pretty good, doesn't it?

How does it work? First you call, make an appointment, and are interviewed by a sales representative. Once the fee is paid, you are put on tape for three to five minutes. You are asked a series of questions, which allows you to put your best foot forward. Some services

help match you up. Others let you pick the number of matches you are entitled to by yourself, based on the bios and videos available for members to examine during office hours. The number of matches you are entitled to will depend on the fee and will vary with the service.

Some video dating services have parties, seminars, and travel programs as additional opportunities for members to meet. Attendance at such functions is generally small, however, because people usually join a video dating service to avoid public activities.

Advantages of Video Dating

By prescreening prospects, you can save time and money. You can check for looks, attitude, quirks, and body language. Poor prospects, who might slip through a screening process using only a picture and a biography, can be eliminated. Prescreening is relatively safe from fraud, as you are required to prove your residence. How many married men want to be filmed? Initial rejection is minimized, because both parties have agreed to get together before either party's name or number is made available. Women and men have equal opportunities to pick and reject prospects.

Disadvantages of Video Dating

Even a video offers a one-dimensional picture — you only see a prospect from the waist up. In addition many desirable propects may summarily reject you, reducing the number of people you can hook up with.

On the other hand, you won't see all of the people who picked you because you may elect to dismiss many of them. In one service that I am familiar with, months went by before a desired prospect received an invitation. Many clients who were viewed stopped using the service after a short time, or rarely made selections.

One service has resorted to a clause in its contract that requires members to come in and preview the video of a member who selected them. If they don't do so within a specified amount of time, their membership is terminated.

Women are at a disadvantage because they often make up more than sixty percent of the membership and, therefore, have fewer options than men using the same service.

The principal users of video dating services are the middle class, the more attractive, and the very selective.

Singles Social Clubs

Another place to find companionship, love and marriage is a singles social club. The requirements for membership vary, as do the fee and the length of membership commitment. Clubs that interview potential members emphasize the care that has been devoted to selecting their members. Other clubs are far less selective.

Social club activities include lectures, parties, dances and comedy nights. Some want a substantial up-front fee and a lower charge per event for members. Clubs that cannot make claims for membership quality and have not prescreened members are most likely to just charge per event.

Your chances of meeting a good prospect depend on the quality and number of singles attending and your ability to meet them. Only fifteen percent of the membership may attend any one activity. Women are more likely to join and attend most functions, making it harder for them to meet a man. Management ought to keep tabs on the male/female ratio, but often they do not.

While nobody likes a rip-off, try to see the plus side of paying dues and fees. If the entrance fee is too low and individuals can pay at the door, a lot of marginal people generally attend. In a short time such an organization can become known as the number one place not to be seen, and it will soon be out of business.

Higher prices, however, don't ensure respectability. I went to check out one social club and was assured that only professional quality singles were admitted. The fee was two hundred fifty dollars for a lifetime membership, plus fees for each activity attended. The offices were dumpy and I was shown an old brochure concealed in a beat-up plastic holder. There were no planned activities for members between Christmas and New Year's, when singles feel most isolated, but the sales office was open. I also discovered that events that were unprofitable for the club were canceled.

Singles social clubs often appear to be better buys than they are because dissatisfied customers seldom complain. A spokesman for the Department of Consumer Affairs in New York City said, "People wouldn't make a complaint, because they feel embarrassed that they went to a dating service at all."

Personal Matchmakers

If you are not meeting enough good prospects, you may consider hiring someone to help you do so. Matchmakers charge anywhere from twenty-five dollars to hundreds of dollars, depending on the quality and the amount of service. Personal matchmakers claim that they will find you good prospects by carefully interviewing candidates and using their knowledge of human behavior to find you matches that will save you time, money and energy.

You have to trust the matchmaker, because the quality of service varies greatly. The matchmaker has to have excellent judgment, provide a sufficient pool of prospects that would be right for you, and be ethical. If you are not satisfied with the service, you have little legal recourse in most states. There is no licensing of matchmakers. As long as you get the number of dates stated in a contract, you can't sue because you didn't like them.

Matchmakers claim they are helping busy professionals conduct their social life in a businesslike manner. Few promise marriage. One matchmaker in New York offers a unique approach. After both candidates agree to meet each other, they are invited to the matchmaker's apartment where the three of them talk briefly over coffee. Then the matchmaker goes to another room, giving the two people a chance to get to know each other. The man and woman then individually report to the matchmaker before leaving the apartment. If there is mutual interest, they go on their first date. If not, they go their separate ways. This kind of approach increases the chances for success, although most matchmakers don't provide this level of personal care.

Singles Weekends

Whether you go on a trip to Club Med or spend a weekend at a hotel, ski lodge, or resort, there will be many opportunities to connect with others. Weekend trips to hotels usually have more, sometimes many more, women than men. Many single weekenders, the majority of whom are women, come home disappointed.

The Ten Keys for Meeting Someone Special on a Weekend

1. Get a private room or share one with a friend who can disappear.
2. Forget the competition.
3. Participate in as many activities as possible—you'll catch up on your sleep at work.
4. If you go with friends, don't spend important meeting time idly chatting with them.
5. Remain positive.
6. Don't get stuck with one person, unless you are sure this is the man or woman you have been looking for, and who is sincerely interested in you.
7. At meal and activity time, park yourself next to members of the opposite sex who interest you.
8. Make sure the person you like is geographically acceptable before you commit yourself.
9. If someone who appeals to you approaches, give him or her a chance.
10. Give your phone number to as many interesting people as you can—you'll screen them on your answering machine later.

As Bob told me: "I went to the Concord Hotel. I played volleyball, some tennis, lived in the pool, ate like a pig, and enjoyed the people at my table. But I didn't meet anyone. How can an engineer with a doctorate, like me, meet a nice girl to settle down with?"

Bob may have been very busy running from one activity to another, but that is not why he went. This scenario doesn't have to happen to you. A weekend can provide more than enough time to meet someone good.

Cruises

Singles cruises are attended principally by women from forty up with some money, but not necessarily with "big bucks." Men have much better chances of meeting someone because of the greater number of women on these cruises. Singles travel organizations or groups only book as many cabins on a particular cruise as they have demand for. The rest of the ship is made up of couples on a cruise—not singles who are cruising. If you are a woman, it will be helpful to use the "meeting naturally" techniques found in this book, or you will spend your time talking to other women or playing bingo.

Cruise tours do have their downside. Since they are put together from any number of organizations and groups, you may find that the man or woman who interests you lives over a thousand miles from your front door.

Special Interest Groups

You name the interest—be it politics, sports, camping or music—and there is a singles organization built around it. Since interests provide a natural bond, you may want to try this route first if you are apprehensive about going out seeking a mate.

If the person you meet shares your passion for foreign films, bird watching, or Eastern philosophy, the least you could do is strike up a lively argument.

Mail Order Love

Many national magazines run personal ads with headlines like "Meet Women World-Wide." Cherry Blossoms has been in business since 1974 and offers to send you a free 32-page catalog. After corresponding for some time, prospects can take a vacation and meet there potential bride in Hong Kong or Thailand. It's not for everyone, but it might be for you.

Rap Groups

One way to get to know someone in a more intimate fashion is to attend a small discussion group commonly known as a rap group. These groups are usually limited to twelve people. The number of groups is determined by the total number of people in attendance. All the people in the group get an opportunity to express their opinions. Sometimes the group picks a topic. Often you can pick a topic from a list and then go to the appropriate group. Before and after your own group activity, you can socialize with members of other groups as well.

Support Groups

Support groups help members adjust and deal with specific difficulties in their lives. Find a support group in your area. If you are recently divorced, for example,

it could be reassuring to meet people in the same
boat. Your peers will help you get your bearings, and
you'll get some leads on how others like yourself
have dealt with similar potholes on the road of life.
And misery loves company; you'll find yourself bonding
quickly and intensely with people who share your
problem.

Getting Personal

Personal ads have become a popular way to make
contact with someone you otherwise wouldn't meet. Ads
can be found in small-town papers as well as national
magazines and periodicals.

Placing an ad has become more acceptable, as more
prestigious publications have begun this kind of advertising. More quality people are taking out and responding to personal ads.

Placing an ad may seem grossly immodest to you,
but it is another way for you to connect with a potential
marriage partner. Some people have met their match
this way, but often after trial periods of disappointments
and rejections reminiscent of job hunting.

Like an employment agency come-on, you are going
to encounter some false advertising.

If you plan to advertise through the personals, it is
best to answer an ad first and see what happens.

Note how people advertise and see if they live up to
their billing. Write out a standard response that can be
easily customized for any ad. Write and address your
letter by hand, using personal stationery.

Once you get comfortable answering ads, you may
want to run an ad on your own.

First, ask yourself what publications your prospective mate is likely to read. Then, read a number of ads in the publication you are planning to advertise in. Next, draft an ad and show it to friends. Be open to criticism and make all necessary adjustments. People will be reading between your lines, as you did when you read others' ads.

Include a brief description of yourself, what you are looking for, and how you can be contacted. Don't be too trusting. End it by requesting a full-length photo.

Touch Tones

You can now meet someone easily by just touching the buttons on your telephone. Modern technology has speeded up the process of meeting. All you have to do is hit the right touch tones and you can dictate your ad or respond to an ad the minute you have read it or check for responses to your ad at any time by just punching in some more touch tones. This technique is known as voice mail.

The two biggest advantages of personal voice mail are that you get to hear the sound of the prospect's voice without speaking to him or her and you don't have to wait a week for a publication to forward your responses.

Answering an electronic personal ad is still a blind date. But these personal ads are a good way to increase your social opportunities without the pain and loss (of time, emotion and money) of the usual blind date.

If you have the option of either writing or leaving a message on voice mail, opt for the letter if you are comfortable writing. Since few people will write, an eloquent letter will truly stand out.

Dining Clubs

Since you have to eat anyway, why not look for a marriage partner at the same time? If you feel comfortable sitting around having dinner and taking in a program, then a singles dinner club may be for you. Religious organizations often provide this type of setting, and their outreach programs will often be geared to singles.

This type of activity tends to attract older, more traditional singles. When you sit down to dine, you are stuck there for the duration of the meal. Too often you realize you could have done better sitting with someone else. Since women outnumber men at such affairs, a woman might find herself two seats away from the nearest man.

It is imperative that you first call the sponsoring organization to check it out. Find out the ratio of men to women and the age breakdowns. Then you can ask if they serve shrimp cocktail.

Remember Dr. Gallatin's prescription for social success: It's not where you go but what you do when you get there.

Activity Review

- ❦ Did you have a good time?
- ❦ Was the admission price acceptable?
- ❦ Was the activity managed properly?
- ❦ Were there enough prospects to choose from?
- ❦ Would you go back again?
- ❦ What did you like best?
- ❦ What did you like least?

Don't Forget The Bars

Bars are a better place to meet your mate than you might believe. When I bring up the topic at seminars, I hear: "Dr. Gallatin, are you kidding? We all know who goes to bars and why."

True, there is probably no social situation where you will feel more self-conscious than in a bar. But if you have some guts you might give bars a chance. Forget about the "meat market" reputation and just try to meet someone.

People do meet their future husband or wife in bars, and don't let anyone tell you otherwise. It's just that few people brag about meeting their mate at a watering hole.

The techniques for meeting someone special in a bar are the same, whether it is your neighborhood tavern or the latest in-spot.

Beating Bar Bias

Too many singles bars are considered pick-up places. This bad rap keeps some serious men, as well as women, away.

It is true that some men go to bars looking for "Miss Goodbod" and a one-night stand. Many men have a number of other things on their minds, however, like finding a steady girlfriend.

We also hesitate to go to bars in the belief that saloons are for desperados, that bar-going singles are desperate for warm bodies.

Exploding Singles Bars Myths

Several myths may be keeping you out of the bars and unnecessarily reducing your social opportunities.

Myth	**Reality**
Men go to bars just for sex.	Men always seem to have sex on their minds, whether they are in a bar, at a dance, or shopping. A man's sexual remark could be ignored or deflected with humor. A man who is truly interested in a woman will not leave because she won't go home with him right then and there. If he is interested only in sex and you are not, just say "No" and speak to someone else.

Unless a women can handle the sexual aspects of flirting, she will have a hard time meeting enough men. A man who doesn't send enough sexual signals may have the worse problem. Women shouldn't make too much out of a man's attempt to be intimate with her, and men shouldn't take a sexual rejection as a personal rejection. In general, there has always been a lot less casual sex in the bar scene than most people realize.

Myth	*Reality*
Bars attract mostly married or unavailable men.	Many eligible single men go to bars because it is easier than pursuing most of the other options in this chapter. Don't worry about "most" of the crowd. A woman needs only to find one man in the entire place who is available and right for her.
You have to be a drinker to go to a bar.	Can you tell the difference between rum and coke and plain coke?
Only losers go to bars.	Nice, respectable people like you *do* go to bars. There are always a few winners, and these are the only men and women you want and need to meet.

The Bars In Town

There are six types of bars:

In-Spots

These are the places where the in-crowd is going. You may have to wait in line, pay top dollar, and be dressed to the hilt—but there will be more worthwhile candidates.

Fern Bars

These bars have lots of greenery and soft lighting. They appeal to women, so you have a better chance of meeting one here.

Commuter Bars

Found near train stations and busy office buildings, commuter bars are used for relaxing before going home. While there is a high proportion of married men, there are also many single men hoping to meet a woman from another office in the area.

Hotel Bars

These bars attract out-of-towners, married men, and those less interested in long-term relationships.

Watering Holes

If you are looking for a local person to date, neighborhood bars can be a good source. In busy areas there will be enough of a turnover to meet a wide variety of people.

Singles Bars

While the pressure is higher, there are many people looking for love. Most singles bars are regular bars that usually cater to singles on Wednesday, Friday, and Saturday nights.

Who You Will Meet

The Winners
Winners dress well, know what they want, and know how to start and end a conversation. They only want to meet other winners.

Neither Here Nor There
The "neither here nor there" are pleasant enough, but are all too forgettable. Talk for as long as you want, then move on. They are wasting their time and yours.

The Desperate
The desperate are driven by their own needs and will often seek you out. Their insistence and desire to continue talking to you can be trying. Quickly end any conversation that you get cornered into.

The Unacceptable
For whatever reason you are not attracted, if someone in this category approaches you, politely say "No" or "No thank you." Discourage that person immediately and firmly.

The Married
A good liar will fool you for a while. But do ask a man directly if he is married. Look right in his eyes and carefully check his reaction.

The Out-of-Towners
You will find out-of-towners principally in hotel and commuter bars. A friendly conversation with appropriate questions should get the truth.

© Maine Line Company, Rockport, Maine.

You Need a Good Attitude

Forget any bad experiences you may have had. Remembering them won't help you to find a mate. A negative attitude in a bar keeps you on the defensive and creates a self-fulfilling prophecy of failure. Taking a quick look around and thinking there is no one here for you will not get you married sooner. A bar is one of the few

places where singles have the opportunity to come and
go at will.

When To Go

It is not a good idea to go to a bar strictly when you
feel in the mood. There are best days to go, usually
Wednesday and Friday. If you go on Saturday night,
you'd better have a thick skin. This doesn't mean you
should not go on Saturday, but it implies that you don't
have a date and, therefore, you may be perceived to be
less desirable.

Gentlemen

Since there are usually many more men looking to
meet a lot fewer women, you must act the moment you
spot someone who interests you. Very few women will
approach you, so resting up against the wall won't work.
If a woman nonverbally expresses an interest, don't
hesitate. She may fear being ignored or rejected by you
and turn toward another man.

Ladies

Bars are packed with men, some of whom you
would like to talk to. Many of these men will hesitate
without some hint of an invitation from you, whether
it be a look at the right moment or a simple request for
a match. The sooner you make contact the greater your
opportunity to meet the best available selection.

Sitting on a stool gossiping with a friend or with
someone who doesn't particularly interest you socially
will not get you the relationship you are seeking. If a

man looks at you and you are interested—smile. If you are close enough, say "hi." Don't end up missing opportunities by not speaking to the men you are attracted to. You are in demand.

Navigating the Bar

- Go when you are in the mood, and on Wednesday or Friday nights.
- Don't expect to fall in love.
- Don't expect to fall into someone's bed and to wake up in love.
- Expect to find at least three good people to talk with.
- Forget the competition.
- Make conversation directly with prospects you are interested in, even if you think it's safer to talk to his or her friend.
- Go with a friend of the opposite sex, if possible.
- Don't let a "No" from one person discourage you from moving on to someone else.
- Circulate. Don't plant yourself on one stool for the duration of your stay.
- Don't think of bars as a last resort. View them as one more place with endless opportunities to be your own matchmaker.

3

What You Want

"It's not only what
you know, but what
you do that counts."

— Dr. Gallatin

53

Getting Started

Picking the right partner is one of the most complex, frustrating and important things you will ever have to do. Most people have less trouble pursuing a career. The difficulties of dating and developing a relationship are underlined by our fifty percent divorce rate.

What you need is an early warning and detection system so that you can eliminate the wrong types without turning away good potential mates.

You want to know immediately who is wrong for you so you don't build up your expectations and get hurt unnecessarily. "Playing the field" only wastes your time, money, and energy. Premarital discrimination is the best system of divorce prevention there is. If the heart leads the head, a marriage is likely to be unsuccessful— whether or not it ends in divorce.

Sometimes we just come across the right person and love follows shortly thereafter. It doesn't often happen this way, though. Most of us have to allow an opening for love just as we have to free the time and energy to pursue that potential love relationship—the one that ought to lead us down the aisle.

Believe it or not, many people will not admit to themselves or to others that they really want to get married. They mistake social and emotional dependency for vulnerability. If the right person came along, though, they would be married in no time flat.

For those of us who are mature enough to consciously pursue marriage, this means developing a love agenda. You have to be as organized and economical as a self-employed businessman. Marriage should be your business. Your social calendar should be as important as your business calendar. Investors don't wait for lottery winnings, and you can't wait for cupid's arrows. We are the ones who bring love into our lives. We consciously do so by looking for someone to love, approaching this person with conversation, and asking for a phone number or follow-through meeting.

Your Love Priorities

If you want romance in your life, you have to know what you want. Your priorities depend on where you are in your life. If you are eighteen, your hormones may still be dictating your priorities. If you are over thirty or divorced after ten long years, it is quite something else. Such people are ready for something as level-headed as an agenda. W. Ruskton Chatsworth III writes in *M Magazine:* ". . . Prince Charles, who before he tied his royal knot once crisply stated, 'If I'm deciding on whom I want to live with for fifty years—well, that's the last decision in which I would want my head to be ruled entirely by my heart'. "

According to Ford Richards of *Gallery Magazine*, "The reason second marriages work is that they usually are planned—just like a business." You may not need or want this much planning.

It is commonly believed that men are the ones who are always hunting for women and they do so in an overly calculating manner. However, Melissa Sands in her book *How to Be a Winner at Love* reports: "Women... are always calculating how to find the best man for them. Yet in spite of all their efforts, women insist that they don't like to play games."

Some people feel more comfortable with a formal agenda that clearly details their objectives and plan of action. Other people need to know where they are going and to be properly motivated but don't need a business plan for their personal lives.

Your agenda is dependent on your personality and your love life. The more you have going for yourself, the less you need to plan how you are going to land a mate. Who knows you better than you, and who knows better what makes you happy?

In deciding on your love priorities you need to consider three things:

a. What do you want to achieve? Do you want to be married or involved in a sustained relationship?

b. When do you want to achieve your goals? Do you want to be married in a year or less?

c. How are you going to get there? What methods of meeting a mate are you willing to try, and in what order?

Love Is Not a Battlefield

Following your priorities should allow you to wrap everything up on schedule. Helen Gurly Brown writes in *Sex and the Single Girl*: "You will have to work your ass off." Dr. Stephin M. Johnson says in *First Person Singular*: "Look upon it [finding a mate] as an important second job."

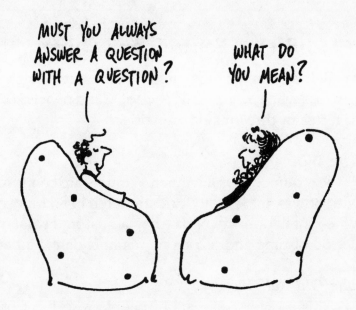

Moonlighting sounds more romantic, but finding a mate shouldn't be all work and no play. There will be some skirmishes and bruises, but love needn't be a battlefield. Just because you have an agenda for your social life doesn't mean that lady luck and mother nature are not at work. Good planning will allow you to be in "the right place at the right time."

Don't Get Stuck

It is easy to get stuck with the wrong person if you feel your choices are limited. You will need determination to move on to new material once you realize it is not working. Staying with the wrong person may be safe, but will only lead to disappointment and tears.

Seeing Yourself and Others

Before you go out there, you'd better honestly appraise who you are. You see people and people see you in terms of three major categories.

The Winner

You cannot miss a winner. Winners are comfortable with others, meet easily, and are often in relationships. When a relationship ends, they adjust in a reasonable period of time and move on. Winners date winners.

The Old Reliable

This category consists of people who meet others fairly regularly, have good relationships, and experience the usual ups-and-downs in their social lives. They do the best they can. When they find someone reasonably compatible, they are willing to settle down, get married, and hope for the best.

The Socially Limited

The socially inhibited have few social skills, are uncomfortable with members of the opposite sex, have a poor self-image, and usually don't know what to do to correct the situation. On the rare occasion that they have a date, the experience just compounds their frustration. Many are "lonatics," or loners who have given up and are reluctant to help themselves.

Who You Want

The best matches are generally made between people who see the world through the same eyes, but have personality differences. An introvert and an extrovert, however, can join to make a fine couple. Opposite personalities attract, but that exotic date from another country, age bracket, race, or religion is not likely to be an ideal spouse. Don't get involved even temporarily with someone who is so different, even though he or she appears exciting. It won't last. You will usually be wasting your time.

It is best to find someone who shares feelings and ideals with you, someone who is equally ready to settle down. A marriage or relationship is jeopardized, for example, when one of you is just beginning to earn a medical or law degree and financial pressure falls on the supporting partner.

No One Around

Some people find that no matter how actively they are looking for romance they rarely spot anyone who interests them. How many times have you been to a party and said or heard someone say, "There is no one here for me." This is often the complaint of a "3" who is looking for a "10." Knowing yourself is essential for success. Date people who are in your league. If you only look for that ideal marriage partner, you may be spending the next few decades by yourself.

You must be able to settle for acceptable candidates in terms of what you have to offer. If you are

UNFORTUNATELY, MOST OF MY MONEY ISN'T LIQUID. IT'S ALL TIED UP IN THINGS LIKE FOOD AND RENT.

exceptionally tall, confined to a wheelchair, or hard of hearing, you are still entitled to happiness and marriage. But you must honestly concede that a person with a similar or different problem could make an acceptable mate.

Never Satisfied

You will run into many people who never seem satisfied. Such people constantly feel that they could be doing better. They not only fail to lower their inflated standards, but they also "would never want to go out with the kind of person who would date them."

The Passive Trap

Too many singles are waiting for something to happen. Many women, especially, dress well, keep their eyes open, and circulate as much as possible. This approach appeals to those people who feel they have a lot to offer but don't believe they have to do anything except get themselves seen. As they age, this approach is less productive. Passivity is a bad habit and a difficult one to break. Only children should be "seen but not heard."

Those who believe they have little to offer are even more afraid to be direct. They are more hurt by rejection. Actually, the less you have to offer, the more active you have to be to get the best possible mate. Most of us need an active love agenda.

Why Women Hesitate to Ask Men

Few women want to actively seek out a man, especially in a public situation. Most women feel that men who are interested in them should make all the moves, under all circumstances. Many women sit around waiting for something to happen. The wait can be long because many men behave the same way.

There are a number of reasons women don't want to make the first move. Women believe that other women and most men will interpret their behavior to be a sign of desperation and lack of desirability. This doesn't have to be the case at all, and if you use the techniques discussed in this book the right way you will not feel uncomfortable quietly signaling your interest. Women who fear rejection are usually overly cautious about approaching a man unless they are absolutely sure he is interested. How many times is one that sure?

If the man you like doesn't approach you first, you can swing into action. The successful approach depends on two things: (1) accepting the idea of taking action yourself; (2) doing so unobtrusively.

When you approach someone you will be met by indifference, loathing, or admiration. The indifferent man won't care one way or the other, so you can forget about him. You may be disappointed, but you shouldn't feel rejected.

Another reaction is loathing. This person doesn't like himself, you, or the world. So why should this person's opinion count for anything?

More commonly, the reaction will reflect admiration. You had the nerve. Whether you succeed or fail to strike up a conversation—or relationship—the man is flattered by your attention and wishes you the best. Even if he didn't think you were his type, he might recommend you to his friends.

Getting Her Man

A woman often has to go after a man who interests her because there are more women than acceptable men in many age categories, creating a disadvantage. Moreover, most women know the type of man they want. Too often the wrong man approaches a woman at a social event and ends up wasting her precious time. A woman must quickly identify the relatively few candidates that meet her standards. Sweetheart, if you don't act, someone else will.

Why Men Don't Approach

Many men hesitate to approach women because they, too, fear rejection. They are even more intimidated by attractive women. Another reason a man won't approach is that he doesn't know what to do under the circumstances. He may spot a woman sitting alone in an ice cream store and not know how to casually start or maintain a conversation. A man may be hesitant to approach if he is not feeling his best or if he is already talking to someone else. He may be interested in a woman, but his feet don't follow his eyes to her corner of the room. Men often fail to make the right moves for various reasons related to their delicate egos.

Your Ideal Marriage Partner

Believe it or not, many people who are looking for their ideal mate don't really know what they want. Fill out my ten-item "Ideal Marriage Partner" profile on the next page and see what you come up with. Did it take you more time to fill in the last five items than the first? The first five are easy. I have looked at thousands of these profiles, and they invariably begin with looks, religious orientation, work preferences, monetary concerns, and geographic area. The order varies more than the content.

It may take a day or so to finalize the ten key qualities you are looking for in a mate. You may attach a color photo of the type of person that physically appeals to you. Then, fill in the approximate height, weight, and age range that you deem acceptable. Put a copy of this profile in your purse or wallet. Its purpose is to motivate you to try harder when you do see someone who may well be ideal for you.

Look at your "Ideal Marriage Partner" profile just before leaving the house in the morning, before going out to lunch, and before retiring to bed. It is a good reminder to carry with you on the way to a singles event. You may want to modify your requirements based on your experiences, so don't treat your profile as if it were carved in stone.

Place Photo of Your Type of Lover Here if You Wish

My Marriage Partner

Height Range:
Weight Range:
Preferred Age Range:

What I Am Looking for in a Marriage Partner:

1. _____

2. _____

3. _____

4. _____

5. _____

6. _____

7. _____

8. _____

9. _____

10. _____

What Women Look For in Men
 Sense of humor
 Sincerity
 Intelligence
 Sensitivity
 Financial security
 Understanding
 Intimacy
 Affection
 Ambition
 Sexiness

What Men Look For in Women
 Sense of humor
 Affection
 Sexiness
 Intelligence
 Sensitivity
 Honesty
 Understanding
 Integrity
 Charm
 Ability to listen

Expect to Do Well

Compare your "Ideal Marriage Partner" profile with the "What I Have to Offer" profile. The sooner the two are compatible, the more you can expect to find your ideal partner. If what you are seeking is too different from what you have to offer, you will have to make a personal reassessment. The more realistic you are, the happier you'll be in the long run.

Don't Get Sidetracked

The way to stay on track is to keep your goals in sight. When you are determined to get what you want, you will learn to take things in stride and live with a certain amount of initial disappointment. But disappointments are merely temporary setbacks. When you don't have a love agenda you will be lonelier and have fewer relationships. Don't let rejection be your constant companion.

Current Social Goals

	YES	NO
❦ To go out more often.	____	____
❦ To meet a wider variety of candidates.	____	____
❦ To go to more different types of activities.	____	____
❦ To have regular dates.	____	____
❦ To date people that are real candidates for marriage.	____	____

Let's Get Emotional

If you decide to carefully select a marriage partner, you don't have to turn your social life into a business proposition. You want to balance your feelings with a sense of reality. We have a tendency to become emotional before we know whether a particular person is good for us. Mutual and lasting love at first sight is all too rare. We have to keep emotions in check until we have checked off our requirements. Carefully pick the best person, then have a compassion explosion. Close your eyes when you kiss, but keep them wide open beforehand.

Time for Love

How much time are you devoting to your social life? Are you allotting it too little or too much? If you devote one night a week to finding a mate, you should have a steady flow of dates.

You can go out by yourself or with friends, but go to places or events that attract the type of person you will be happy with. Since you should be interacting with potential mates in the course of your everyday life, dedicating one night a week to attending social events should give you more than enough time for meeting new people.

Holding the Hands of Time

If you are over thirty and want a child, you may hear the biological clock ticking away. (While men can still father children in their forties and fifties, they want to be young enough to play ball with their sons.) You will have to consciously follow your love priorities or you may become obsessed, depressed, and feel compelled to settle for someone you'll later regret having married.

The older you are, the sooner you need to begin implementing your plan. While it may be easier if you are younger, it is never too late.

Lover Profile

Get to know yourself and the history of your love life. Know who you are looking for and what you have to offer. How consistent are you in dating the type of person who is best for you? Does your current or former lover fit into your "Ideal Marriage Partner" profile? If not, are you afraid to get involved with this type of person? Even if you have a long and troubled track record behind you, there is no reason not to do better.

Meeting...
Wherever You Are

**"You never know who
you will meet, nor
where or when."**

— Dr. Gallatin

Meeting Naturally

If you want to be married in a year or less, you need to use the same techniques employed by people with successful relationships and marriages. As useful as you may have found Chapter Two, "Going Out," most people meet a mate on their own, in the normal course of their everyday lives.

While singles activities and introduction services do provide opportunities to make connections and dates, a minority of these relationships actually result in marriage. Weren't some of your best dates and relationships the result of using your own resources?

Wherever you go, you see people you would like to meet. Just because you're at a bus stop or supermarket doesn't mean you should let these opportunities pass you by. Meeting naturally while shopping or attending a computer class shouldn't intimidate you.

People hesitate to meet naturally because they don't know how to pull it off. One can learn by participating in a *How to Get Married in a Year or Less* seminar that demonstrates techniques for meeting naturally wherever you are. You can practice the art of meeting naturally in a supportive environment that allows you to observe what you are especially good at and encourages self-improvement.

While it is all right for men to "pick up" women, women find it hard to comfortably "hit on" a man. Dr. Gallatin's tips allow both women and men to meet anyone, anywhere, any time. Results come from following the guidelines.

The great thing about meeting naturally is that you don't have to wait for someone to call for a date or schedule a singles event. You can be your own matchmaker anytime you see someone who interests you, and you don't have to dress up or pay admission.

Most singles prefer to meet wherever they are. They feel that their chances of successful encounters are greater, and if a meeting doesn't work out, the embarrassment is minimal. On a bank line, unlike a singles event, there is no pressure to come away with a phone number or date.

When meeting naturally, rejection is a private thing. At a party or a singles bar an unsuccessful advance feels like striking out in the World Series. Discussing a tie or the latest phone answering machine at a department store, however, doesn't publicize the fact that you are trying to meet someone. If that someone is not interested, the "rejection" will be a simple "I have to get going now."

The common belief that it is more difficult to meet naturally is reinforced when we occasionally try and it doesn't work out. You need to have reasonable expectations. You also must be able to present yourself effectively in a very short time. With practice you will be amazed at how well you can do. Your "chance" conversations will last longer and you will soon get the desired results. Instead of self-doubt you will feel self-confidence.

Meeting naturally should be a normal part of your daily life. When we come across someone interesting in a library, adult education class, or record store, we often act indifferent or busy when in reality we are anxious to begin a new relationship. We are afraid of making our interest seem too obvious. It presents quite a problem to meet if someone who may be interested in you thinks you are unapproachable. Research demonstrates clearly that women who don't adequately signal men will meet fewer of them. Men must be aware that women dropping handkerchiefs or books in their path are cliches of the past and not the methods by which they will be given the green light to proceed.

Roadblocks to Meeting Anywhere

Let us look at the main roadblocks to meeting naturally and see how they can be overcome.

Roadblock	*What To Do*
I don't know if the person is available.	Barring a wedding ring, the only way to find out is to talk. Women often mention directly or indirectly if they are not available. When you ask for a phone number or drop a reference to a potential boyfriend, girlfriend, or spouse you will find out with a minimum of embarrassment.

What if the other person realizes that I am flirting?

If you act correctly in the particular situation, you won't have any problem. If the person is interested in you, he or she will be glad. If not, you will only have a moment of embarrassment when the person mutters something and walks off.

The person may try to take advantage of me.

No one can take advantage of you unless you allow it.

How can I get the conversation started and keep it going?

Use any of the techniques discussed in Chapter Six and you will do well.

How do I make the transition from a business situation to a social one?

Use any of the techniques found in Chapter Nine.

What do I do if I spot someone on a bus or elevator or other situation where I won't see him or her again five minutes later?

Under these conditions your skills have to be very sharp. Do your best to sound natural while offering an opportunity for a follow-up call or meeting.

It's Mother Nature's Way

The major advantages of meeting naturally are:

- ❧ It is comfortable and uncontrived.
- ❧ People are more themselves.
- ❧ The number of places to make contact is limited only by your imagination, life-style, personality, and expectations.
- ❧ You can act according to your mood.
- ❧ You can try all the techniques and see which ones work best for you without being limited to certain times and places.
- ❧ Meeting can occur in your neighborhood, at work, or anywhere.
- ❧ No one will know but the person with whom you are talking.
- ❧ You always have uncontrived topics to begin conversations with.
- ❧ You never have to wait for a singles event or social occasion.

Where to Meet

There is no best place to meet quality men or women. You really don't need a list of special locations. The best place to meet someone is wherever you happen to see a person that you like. The number of opportunities you will have is determined by your life-style and personality more than anything else.

Here is a sample of places and activities where a person may meet someone with common interests.

Dr. Gallatin's Top 10 Ways to Meet a Mate

1. Through friends
2. On supermarket lines
3. Shopping at the mall
4. At work
5. On the dance floor
6. At the bar
7. Attending quality singles functions
8. During sporting events
9. Participating in religious, community and
   political activities
10. While commuting or traveling

Some Natural Opportunities

shopping malls
sporting events
newsstands and bookstores
business conventions
libraries
street fairs
religious activities
department stores or shopping malls
walking a dog
auctions
amusement parks
planes or airports
trains
company cafeterias
job or apartment hunting
restaurants and coffee shops
museums
jury duty
ice cream parlors
bowling alleys
office parties
video stores
taking a tour
hardware stores
standing in line at a bank or movie
supermarkets and convenience stores
volunteering in a hospital or social service
craft fairs
using your camera
teaching a course or giving talks

apartment building or neighborhood committees
public holiday celebrations
adult education courses
watching street entertainers
film clubs
vending machines
laundromats
professional or political organizations
selling door to door or in a store
health food stores
hiking and camping groups
health clubs
admiring window displays
outdoor art exhibits
large public events or demonstrations

Sizing up a Natural Opportunity

Before you act, ask yourself these questions:

❦ Are you in the mood and looking right?

❦ Is the person alone?

❦ Would the person be caught at an awkward moment?

❦ Does the person appear to be a good possibility for you?

❦ Is there enough time to get a conversation going?

Be Chosen

While there is no reason why you can't meet whoever you want, wherever you are, whenever you feel like it, the ideal situation is to be chosen by someone who really turns you on. When you do spot someone special you don't always have to walk right up and introduce yourself. Let your body language and voice project receptiveness. Place yourself in a position where you could be approached. The air that you project will magnetically attract that one interesting man or woman. When someone strikes your fancy and the feeling is mutual phone numbers will be exchanged, dates will follow and marriage may be only months away.

Dr. Gallatin's Eight Steps to Be Married in a Year or Less

1. Visualize your marriage partner.
2. Know yourself and what you have to offer.
3. Actively seek and date marriageable prospects.
4. Set a deadline for each person.
5. Use sensible dating skills.
6. Make the relationship work.
7. Say "Yes" or propose at the right time.
8. Plan your wedding and honeymoon.

If you follow these eight steps, I guarantee you will be happily married in a year or less. Until you have decided that you are going to get married, you will retreat to the serenity of your own home or into the arms of someone who won't marry you whenever you encounter any difficulty. You must carefully follow these steps and suggestions, no matter how obvious they appear or what attempts you have already made to find a marriage partner. The more optimistic you are, the sooner you will get down the aisle of romance, love and marriage.

If you are not married within a year or less from your reading of this book, then you are not following the advice systematically enough. Experience has taught me that the following behavior patterns keep people from being married in a year or less.

• Relying too much on luck.
• Spending too much energy on detailed planning rather than on action.
• Doing things your own way because it seems right.
• Being negative.
• Not giving situations appropriate time.
• Not accepting rejection and moving on.

Step No. 1
Visualize Your Marriage Partner

In order to attract the best mate you have to know who you want to marry. You may know the type that turns you on and you may not. If you know your type move on to step two. If you are not sure, you need to find out before you accept another date. I recommend you go to a room where you feel comfortable and where you won't be bothered. Take off your watch, turn on your answering machine and have paper and pencil available. Put on some soothing background music, close your eyes and think of the individuals you have gone out with who have made you the happiest. Next, think of those dates and relationships that didn't work. Take the pad and draw a line down the center. On the left side write what will make me happy and on the right side write what won't. List ten things in each category. Now transfer the things that will make you happy to your ideal marriage partner list.

Now you know what you are looking for and what to stay away from. You may want to do this visualization process several times. If your relationships aren't working out, you'll need to revise your list.

Step No. 2
Know Yourself
And What You Have To Offer

The better you know your strengths and your limitations, the sooner you will be married to your first choice. You will also need to know who you can realistically get and be happy with.

Fill in the ten most important things you have to offer on the "Go with your strengths" list. You won't live up to your potential until you are aware of how much you have to give. When you know what you have to offer, you can confidently introduce yourself to anyone or be at your best when you are approached unexpectedly.

Don't voluntarily bring up your limitations, but do know how to work around them.

Step No. 3
Actively Seek and Date
Marriageable Prospects

If you want to be married you need to be going out with your type who is available. Sometimes luck and divine intervention will help you meet your match, but most of the time you have to discreetly seek opportunities. You may respond to a personal ad or quietly say hello at just the right moment. Sitting at home alone or gossiping with friends over the phone while lounging in your pajamas won't get you married.

Step No. 4
Set a Deadline for Each Person

To get married in a year or even less you must find out as quickly as possible whether a person you are seeing is for you. This is not always easy. The minute you realize that your date is not someone you could marry you have to end it, as painful as it may be. You're not looking for friends. Be gentle but firm. You might say, for example, "Bill, this is a little hard for me to say, but we just don't have enough in common for it to work romantically. I wish you all the best." When he tries to change your mind say, "I realize you want to continue seeing me and are disappointed, but it's better for both of us to know where we stand. You'd make a fine friend, but I'm looking for a marriage partner." You will feel a little bad, but you'll realize you have done the right thing.

For each romantic possibility, allow up to five dates to decide if you should continue to see this person. Having a deadline will prevent you from getting emotionally involved with the wrong person. While you don't have time to waste on the wrong person, you have plenty of time for the right one. Give each possibility a real chance.

When we get too involved too soon, the thought of starting all over is distressing. But staying with the wrong person isn't the easy way out. It is hard to look for someone else when you are emotionally involved, even if your current affair won't lead to marriage.

Step No. 5
Use Sensible Dating Skills

In order to be successful, you need to use appropriate dating skills to meet as well as to develop a permanent relationship. (I offer you 27 of the most important ones.) We will be going over these tips one at a time. Some of them you are good at and some of them you could brush up on.

Step No. 6
Develop And Make
The Relationship Work

Someone who is "good for you" meets your physical, emotional and intellectual requirements and provides you with all the love you want. The relationships that work the best are the ones where each person has the same way of looking at things, but have personality differences. Only get emotionally involved with someone who has a history of positive relationships. Make sure Mr. Right is not wrong for you by first finding out what you need to know. Don't hesitate to ask key questions. When you ask questions at the right moment you will get your answer. You don't have to know every little thing about the person's past but you must know the significant things.

In today's increasingly complex world couples have to make a continuous effort to make the relationship work. If you are holding out for the perfect relationship you will never get married.

Step No. 7
Say "Yes" or Propose
at the Right Time

After you have been seeing each other for six months or so, it's "go or no go," depending on your age and circumstances. Either you are going to get married or you're not. Being in love and sending strong non-verbal signals isn't enough. You need to make your intentions clear—in words—and make a commitment. If you are younger or if there are reasons why you cannot get married as soon as you would like, you can commit yourself to marriage with a long-term engagement. While you have not tied the knot officially (because of that degree, promotion, or down payment) you are a committed couple who engaged to marry at a specific time. If you are older and economically secure there should be no excuse for not picking a reasonably early date.

No matter how much someone likes you, you don't know if she will marry you until you pop the question. Some women, once they are divorced, never allow a man to get too close—even if they are sleeping together. Love and sex are not grounds for marriage in everybody's mind.

If a man is hesitant to ask for a woman's hand in marriage, she can give him a gentle push to the altar. Many men need a little encouragement to propose, especially the first time. A woman might say, "Charlie, we have been seeing each other for six months and you know how much I love you and I know you feel the same way. I would appreciate it if you could tell me if we have a future trogether?"

If you don't get a clear commitment, you should try again. Then, if the answer is, "I am not ready" or "I need more time" it is up to you to decide whether you want to stay for a while or walk away while you still can.

Step No. 8
Plan Your Wedding
And Honeymoon

All you have to do now is to begin drawing up your wedding plans and to decide whether you are going to spend your honeymoon in Rio or the Rockies. Good luck! I am looking forward to receiving your wedding invitation.

Dr. Gallatin's Tips for Meeting Anyone, Anywhere, Anytime

In order to achieve the best results, use Dr. Gallatin's guidelines. The tips have all been tested in the field at department stores such as Bloomingdale's, at shopping malls and supermarkets throughout the country, and at singles activities nationwide. In addition, the author shares data that have been carefully gathered through years of offering *How to Get Married in a Year or Less* seminars.

Dr. Gallatin's Tips

- Assess the field and identify your three best prospects.
- Approach the best available person immediately.
- Politely end conversations when prospects prove undesirable; go on to another person.
- Aim for three good phone numbers during an extended singles event.
- Always have a pen and a card handy.
- Assume the person you approach will be interested in you.
- Show genuine enthusiasm.
- Be positive.
- Smile.
- Size up the person.
- Talk to be remembered.
- Act appropriately for each place and crowd.
- Use humor for openers or to deflect anxiety.
- Open with small talk.
- Dress well.
- Concentrate on one possibility at a time; don't talk to one person while eyeing another.

❦ Look for signs of interest.
❦ Circulate.
❦ Don't be sexually preoccupied.
❦ Together, you and I.
❦ Find a common ground fast.
❦ Be accepting.
❦ Sound fresh.
❦ Stay on track.
❦ Entertain.
❦ Don't surprise anyone.
❦ Talk to more than one.

Pick Three Possibilities

You cannot talk to everyone, and you don't want to. Review your "Ideal Marriage Partner" profile to more effectively narrow down the field and better use your time.

A party or club with many people can be overwhelming. Check your coat, have a drink in your hand (it can be mineral water), and position yourself to see everyone in the area clearly and comfortably. Now carefully look at all the members of the opposite sex to see who you could meet. Pick the three that interest you the most, based on your overall impression of each person. Try to speak to the choices in the order that you selected them. If none of the three is available, speak to a fourth, fifth, or sixth choice. The moment one of your three candidates becomes available, politely withdraw from your conversation and go right over.

If the setting involves a large group, follow the same procedure after dividing a crowded room into manageable areas.

When you pick three possibilities you are motivated to act and be at your best, because the three candidates you have selected really interest you. You need to look at everyone, thereby increasing the chances of finding someone who interests you. You know exactly who you want to talk to. You also know the order in which you want to talk to the three people chosen. You should always try to reduce the number of people in a room or area, regardless of the crowd, to three. You will be comfortable using this approach because three people is a manageable number. Most social situations should afford you the opportunity to find three candidates to talk with. If you rarely find that many people who interest you, it may be that you are not looking carefully enough. You may be far too discriminating, or perhaps you are going to the wrong places.

Approach the Best Available Person Immediately

Make your way over to the person you want to talk to as soon as possible—he or she may leave or hook up with someone else. Your first impression is usually correct. Don't wait for a positive reaction or a return glance—it may not be his or her style. Back off only if you feel you are getting negative body language.

Avoid Dead-End Conversations

Know how to ask for a number or to say good-bye within twenty minutes. Don't waste your valuable time talking to someone because you feel obligated to carry on a conversation. Break off politely, though, as you may bump into this person again.

You may want to use a closing phrase like "It was nice speaking with you," "Enjoy the (evening, afternoon, party, etc.)" or "Take care of yourself. I have to get going."

Get Three Numbers

Anyone can collect phone numbers at a party or social affair. But if you get three good numbers from potential mates, you have a better chance for something to develop.

Inevitably, one of the men or women who gave you a number will end up getting back together with a former lover or will look far less appealing under brighter lights. Having three numbers, then, gives you two backup opportunities.

Have a Pen and a Card Handy

Be prepared to write a name and number down. Your memory may fail you under the pressure of a singles event or the time contraints of a supermarket line.

I was on a bus in Manhattan where new acquaintances almost remained strangers because of unpreparedness. Just before the man had to get off the bus, the woman he had just met rummaged through her bag looking for a pen and paper. The poor guy was also without a pen or business card. They had to settle for a crumpled piece of newspaper from the floor and a phone number scratched on with an eyeliner pencil.

When you are ready to ask for a number, you can say: "I really enjoyed talking with you. Let's exchange home numbers and talk again." As you begin asking for a phone number, take out your pen and a business or personal card with your name printed on it. If you don't have either card, here's a good reason to get some.

Based on your impression of the person asking (or the proximity of your immediate supervisor) you can decide whether you want to give out your home number, your work number, or both.

Have a place in your pocket or purse where you can quickly reach in and unobtrusively get out your card and pen when you need them. If you are not prepared, you lose opportunities and come across like a scatterbrain.

Assume the Person Will Be Interested

When you start talking with someone, assume that he or she will be genuinely interested in spending a few minutes with you. Focus on having a pleasant conversation. If you are anticipating a bad experience or expecting to be rejected, your insecurity will show through and you'll greatly increase the probability of failure.

Show Genuine Enthusiasm

One of the best ways to sustain someone's interest is to show enthusiasm with your voice, gestures, and attitude. Enthusiasm is contagious. Acting enthusiastic is a way of demonstrating interest without saying: "You are just the person I have been looking for"—which is not quite appropriate at this point.

Be Positive

Too many singles begin talking to a stranger with a negative approach. Take Hank. He walks up to women at dances and asks: "Why aren't you dancing?" A better approach is: "The music sounds great; let's dance to this one."

Being negative doesn't encourage interest; rather it reinforces negative feelings. When one is positive, it is more difficult for the other person to be negative or to say "No."

From the moment you begin talking to someone, your whole being has to project: "I am interested in talking to you and I am receptive to what you have to say." It is no more work to be positive than to be negative. Being negative is just a bad habit, which you can change.

Smile

Whether you approach someone or you are being approached—smile. Your smile will create a bond without your having to say a word. Even if you are caught by surprise and you are not sure of your interest—smile. You can always wipe the smile off if an ogre or ogress is after you, but a pleasant, natural smile creates a sense of comfort and friendliness.

Size Up the Person

From the moment you spot someone and begin talking, you should be assessing the kind of person he or she is. Don't whip out your copy of this book; rather compare the person to your "Ideal Marriage Partner" profile.

Talk to Be Remembered

If you just talk to hear yourself talk or to maintain a conversation, you won't come off as a desirable or even interesting person. Avoid cliches "like the plague." Choose dramatic words and phrases, using your own natural style. Give the listener a distinct sense of who you are and what interests you. Use the conversational techniques discussed in Chapter Six.

Act Appropriately

Before you open your mouth, see if the setting is formal and reserved, or relaxed and casual. Check the mood and age range of the crowd. How you present yourself and how you speak should depend on who you are with. So look around and be sure to get a sense of where you are.

Use Humor

Humor is one of the best ways to win favorable attention. It will get one relaxed and his or her lower their guard. Humor allows you to ask and say things you would not normally get away with. Your humor should flow naturally and spontaneously; don't come with prepared lines or routines. The clown will get laughs, but no dates. An average-looking man or woman with a genuine sense of humor will attract the best people available.

Open with Small Talk

Small talk can really be big talk. Never put down small talk. When two strangers meet, whether at a singles dance or a bookstore, both need a little time to size each other up before making any serious overtures. Small talk gives each party a little necessary breathing room. People who are not comfortable with small talk may feel that they are just not good at it. Too much intensity too early will most often scare people away.

Those who open conversations with something heavy are much more likely to feel rejection when their listeners beg off.

Dress Well

The first thing that someone notices about you is how you dress and look. Sure it may sound shallow, but what else do we have to go on? We don't dress by accident but by design. Most people are not experts in judging others by body language, so they often react to a person's clothes. Dressing well and appropriately will enhance your desirability. Dressing well does not require a six-figure salary. If you have limited funds, you can select a few quality outfits that can be effectively mixed and matched.

One at a Time

When you start talking with someone, concentrate all your attention on that person until you decide to move on. Look directly at the person and take in all the small but important details. You'll increase your chances of accurately sizing up this prospective mate. The person will notice and be flattered by your attention.

Look for Signs of Interest

When you are speaking with someone who particularly attracts you, watch to see if the person is responding with some interest. If you are taking a stranger by surprise, there may be little or no initial interest. Developing signs of interest include moving somewhat closer, smiling, and chatting in a more conversational manner. Women can often act more interested than they are because they tend to be more polite.

Circulate

Getting noticed by good catches will not just happen if you hide in the corner. Act as if your uncle owns the place and stay as long as you're enjoying yourself. Just pay attention to those people you want to get to know and work yourself into their line of vision. While you don't want to cause a scene, you don't want to become a part of the scenery. So stand front and center; leave the security of the walls for the wallflowers.

Don't Be Sexually Preoccupied

Many singles don't look for a mate until their sexual urges become overwhelming. Then they go out hunting instead of looking. One-night stands only become life-time partners in the movies. Never go food shopping when you're hungry; never go out looking for love when you're horny.

Together, You and I

Think of the person you are meeting as your friend, not as a stranger. Don't see the other person as someone you have to overwhelm, but rather as someone enjoyable to talk to for as long as you both like. Center your attention more on the other person than on yourself. Each of you may desire companionship, and this may be a common bond.

I'M LOOKING FORWARD TO MEETING YOU TOO, LOU. LET'S JUST HOPE YOU'RE NOT A TOTAL DISAPPOINTMENT.

Find a Common Ground

You have to make a stranger feel comfortable with you, so you should talk long enough to discover if both of you are interested. Quickly find out what the other person's interests are and take it from there. With more anxious people, it is particularly important to get on familiar ground. He or she will more likely loosen up and get comfortable when discussing French cooking, tax laws, or music of the fifties.

Be Accepting

The more openness you project, the more a stranger will open up to you. You may find out about a previous marriage in only ten minutes instead of three dates later. Be wary of implying any criticism, as first encounters are rife with oversensitivity. Make encouraging comments without resorting to phony compliments.

Sound Fresh

You may have to make a conscious effort not to sound mechanical when repeating something about yourself to the tenth person in three hours. Your motivation to sound fresh is that the next person you talk to could become your mate. Let each person's personality inspire you to freshness.

Stay on Track

When you meet someone new, your objective is to discover who the person is—not just to have an interesting conversation. Don't fall into the trap of talking about yourself. You're wasting your time and sounding egotistical. Guide the discussion so that you are finding out the information you need to know about this potential mate. You're on a reconnaissance mission; don't just admire the scenery.

Entertain

Give the person you are with a good reason to keep talking with you. Become a good storyteller, work those eyebrows, vary your intonation—keep that someone's attention. With practice, you can make ordinary things sound extraordinary. It is not necessary to be a professional actor. As John D. Rockefeller, Sr. said, "Take the common and make it uncommon."

Don't Surprise Anyone

When you approach a person make sure that he or she sees you before you get too close. Women, especially, may be frightened if a man they don't know is suddenly eighteen inches in front of them, making an unsolicited comment or asking a question. People caught by surprise are more apt to be concerned with regaining their composure or escaping than with listening to you. Surprise doesn't make for a good first impression. Walk up at a normal pace, look at the person straight in the eyes, and give him or her every opportunity to see you approaching.

Talk To More Than One

The reality is that you have to talk to an incredible number of people who appear to have potential before you find one that has what you are looking for. When we do meet a good prospect, we too often stop searching for someone else. This is likely to be a mistake since so many things can and do go wrong in relationships. Reach out to several potential mates. You will learn a lot about people and maybe something about yourself.

Keep These in Mind

The following points are worthy of your special attention:

Walk Out on Rejection

If you get or sense rejection—just gracefully move on. Your disappointment will fade when you are busy with a new and, it is hoped, better person. If you consciously or subconsciously think too much about rejection, you'll be too upset to act. See Chapter Seven for a full discussion of rejection.

It Doesn't Matter Where or How You Meet Someone

There is no right time or place to meet someone. Think in terms of people, not places. Why does it matter if you meet someone while on your coffee break, at a phone booth, at a dance, or at a bar? We often meet new people when we least expect it. If you concentrate on meeting someone at a particular place and under very specific circumstances, you are greatly reducing your chances of success. You are also reducing your chances of meeting people on the spur of the moment.

Availability

Even if someone readily talks with you, it doesn't mean he or she is interested in you romantically. Some people are naturally friendly or talkative. The person might simply want to see if you find him or her attractive, but may not be trying to socially connect with you in any way.

To determine if someone is available for you, try to find out if the person is really interested in meeting someone and getting married at this time. See if the person is financially prepared for marriage and, more importantly, emotionally prepared? Perhaps you'll discover that he or she has just come out of a messy divorce or just ended a long love affair. These people are still healing. If they were to get involved right away, while "on the rebound," the relationship could be a precarious one.

A man or woman just out of a long marriage is usually more interested in casual dating rather than any heavy relationship. These people might be using you

"I met my first husband at Bloomingdale's and my second husband at Banana Republic."

Drawing by Dana Fradon; © 1986 The New Yorker Magazine, Inc.

during their transition time of adjustment. I'd say ditto for a widow or widower in the first year of bereavement. On the other hand, a man or woman who has never married should not be dismissed even if that person is pushing fifty. Nobody has to be a playboy, playgirl, bachelor, or old maid for life. For various reasons, these people may have postponed marriage but now may be fully ready.

Many of this chapter's principles and guidelines are embodied in the seminar, "Lover Shopping at Bloomingdale's." The Course Description and Program from the seminar are represented here.

Lover Shopping at Bloomingdale's

This three-hour seminar will show you what you need to know to attract a mate. You will be given an opportunity to try out what you have learned and to receive coaching on how to do your best.

The first hour takes place in a classroom setting where you are supplied with the specific techniques. Questions will be answered before we proceed to the store itself for an hour of putting theory into practice.

Students are encouraged to approach interesting people that they'd like to meet. They will try to let innocent questions (for example, "Pardon me, which of these ties goes best with a dark suit?") evolve into a conversation—and perhaps more.

The seminar ends at a local pub where, over drinks, we discuss our experiences and get to meet the fellow participants.

5

&

The Available You

"If you act like
everyone else, you
will end up like
everyone else."
— Dr. Gallatin

On The Shelf

As a single, you want potential mates to quickly get a sense of you. You want to quickly and accurately evaluate people yourself. While you cannot tell a book by its cover, you can learn to scan a cover and skim a book to find out if it's worth reading.

You are like a book on the shelf. You want to attract browsers as if to say, "Here I am, pick me up and read me." You want to attract favorable attention.

Aside from attending an organized singles activity, some of your best social prospects will catch you by surprise. You may be at the deli in your jeans or at the video shop selecting a movie. Attracting favorable attention and being able to respond naturally should become second nature.

Whether you are center stage at a party or having a sandwich in the school cafeteria—you have to be prepared to meet potential mates, but you don't always have to be looking.

The Real You

The more familiar you are with your real self, the more confidence you'll have and the better prepared you will be to meet anyone, anytime, in the most natural and spontanous way.

You needn't pretend to be something you are not. You should also attempt to see others for what they really are.

If you think you are good at sniffing out a phony in a crowd of singles—that pretender trying to act cultured, rich, popular or sexy—then look into a mirror to be sure that you are not putting on any masks. Ask your closest friends or relatives for an honest appraisal or seek professional help if you are having trouble getting through to the real you.

The first time you kissed someone, how did it feel? Was it totally natural? While you might have enjoyed it, you probably focused too much on the execution and reception of the kiss. After more experience, your confidence surely increased. You responded more naturally, became more creative, and increased the satisfaction of both parties. Just as your kissing got better, so will your social skills. The key is self-confidence, which has everything to do with self-knowledge.

Getting Flustered

Salespeople and trial lawyers may on occasion be at a loss for words. This may happen to you precisely at the wrong time—when you are about to talk to that attractive stranger. Don't dwell on your temporary failure. Take advantage of your vulnerability by showing the person how human and how sincere you really are. It can be an asset to admit that you're nervous.

On the Tip of Your Tongue

While at a social event you will inevitably be asked the same questions over and over. You may get irritated, forgetting that the person asking doesn't know you. Keep your responses short and to the point; the interested prospect is not concerned with every single word but with the overall feeling that you convey.

You may be tempted to ask preliminary questions that sound too much like cliches. The most successful conversationalists are careful not to bore anyone with standard inquiries. Try some of the following alternatives:

Most Commonly Asked Questions	*Recommended Alternatives*
Do you come here often?	Do you know the host hostess/management/ speaker?
What do you do for a living?	I like your suit. Are you coming straight from work as I am?
Have you ever been married?	You are too nice to be a single so long. I'll bet you're a...When the right person comes along I would like to be married. What has your experience with marriage been like?
Do you have any children?	I'm sorry to hear that about your marriage. Were there any children involved?

How come you
aren't/have never
been married?

You certainly seem like
good marriage material.
What kept you from
tying the knot?

Where did you grow up?

I'm trying to place that
charming accent, where
did you grow up?

Love on the R Train Patti Dell was
not looking for romance. Not on the R train to
Queens, at any rate.

Last year, Ms. Dell, an aspiring opera singer
with a full-time job in fund-raising, moved
from Manhattan to Queens. One morning as
she was riding the R to work, she spotted a
handsome man in a trench coat.

She began to see him regularly, hoping
every day that he would turn up on her train.
She knew she was staring at him, but she drew
the line at speaking to him.

"I didn't want to be a pushy New York
woman," she said.

Then one morning after six months of this,
as they got out at Times Square, he said, "How
are you?" That did it.

He told her his name was Todd Ortone and
that he was in fund-raising — which seemed to
both of them a terrific coincidence. He invited
her to the restaurant at the top of the Marriott
Hotel — "There was a clear sky and full
moon," she recalled — and he told her that he
had been waiting a long time for the right moment to say something. He had thought about
dropping a note in her lap while they were
aboard the subway but didn't.

"He wanted to be sure I wouldn't shun him,"
she said.

Patti Dell and Todd Ortone are now engaged
and plan to be married next year.

"My mother always told me it was rude to
stare, but I'm glad I didn't listen to her this one
time," Ms. Dell said happily.

Deirdre Carmody

What You Have to Offer

Everyone has some traits, physical or psychological, that enhance their social success. The key to winning is knowing how to emphasize your strengths and minimize your limitations. The more you have going for you, the more choices you have. It is easy to want the best, but you get what you pay for—what you offer in your own assets. This is known as the parity principle.

Use Your Strengths

Sometimes we don't realize how much we have to offer or we are a little too hesitant to show our strengths.

Everyone has some qualities that others find desirable and that make us feel good about ourselves. Fill out the "What I Have to Offer" profile, so you can focus on your personal strengths. Draw up a list. Have a good friend check your list and add some qualities that you may have left out.

What I Have to Offer

1. _____
2. _____
3. _____
4. _____
5. _____
6. _____
7. _____
8. _____
9. _____
10. _____

Now ask yourself if you are effectively displaying your strengths to propective mates. Perhaps you should be seen more often in a bathing suit. Maybe you should go to parties and talent shows where your piano playing can be heard. If you're a better talker than dancer, get away from noisy discos. If you are great with children, offer to meet his or her kids at a picnic.

What's Missing?

Everyone has some characteristics that potential mates will find undesirable. You don't need to eliminate all of your drawbacks to be successful with members of the opposite sex. You should certainly not dwell on flaws that you can't correct. Don't make excuses for your limitations. Improve what you can, then go forward to find the best mate you can.

HAVEN'T I SEEN YOU SOMEPLACE BEFORE?

What you consider to be a serious disadvantage may not be for many prospective mates. Take height, for example. Many men prefer taller women, while tall women are often needlessly embarrassed by their height. Likewise, many average or short women are more comfortable with a man they don't have to look up to, while shorter men are often unnecessarily upset about their size.

Some Common Disadvantages	How to Minimize Them
You are not married and never have been.	Tell prospect that you are now ready to spend the rest of your life with the right person. Don't make excuses for your past.
Live far away from prospect.	Tell prospect she or he is worth it and you will work it out. Solutions include meeting halfway and rotating the travel.
Overweight.	Begin a formal weight-reduction program.
Too tall.	Find someone who prefers tall partners. Short men can like tall women and vice versa. You will only find out by raising the issue with someone.

Serious medical condition; for example, asthma.	Maintain a cheerful attitude. Tell prospect at the appropriate time, "My medical condition is a fact, but I don't let it rule my life."
Inhibited/ self-conscious.	Find a companion to go places with. Follow the suggestions and ideas in this book carefully. Attend activities with small to medium-sized groups and work up to more challenging affairs.
Low status job.	Make no excuses. Confidently say, "This is what I do for a living." Develop yourself into the most interesting person possible. If you are rejected because of the kind of work you do, find someone else.
Less attractive than some other people.	Make yourself as attractive as possible. If a woman, make sure your makeup enhances your looks. Everyone should get the best haircut for their features. Dress for your body, build, and figure. If need be, find a wardrobe consultant.

Gaining Favorable Attention

When you initially meet someone, you want to capture the person's imagination for a few minutes. Then you can both decide if you want the conversation to evolve into a future meeting or a date. The more you use the following keys, the more romantic doors you'll be able to open.

Dress and Look Interesting

Let's face it, next to your physical appearance, the first thing anyone notices is how you dress. And the way we dress is no accident. Our clothes must send the right message to the right people. How much money you spend is less important than how you spend it.

Treat the Person You Are Talking to as Unique

Look directly at your prospect for as long as you are interested. Sound like you have never said whatever you are saying before. Don't think of anyone or anything else.

Choose Your Words and Content Carefully

Avoid obscure references to things in your field. You may think you're impressing someone, but you're boring your prospective mate. Your accounting prowess, for instance, may mean nothing to someone who doesn't know a debit from a credit. Don't just say anything that happens to come to mind. Don't use four-letter words. Most women don't like foul language, especially from men they don't even know. Men often view the use of four-letter words by women as unfeminine, as a sign of poor breeding, or as a sexual come-on.

Make sure you say enough. If your answers are too brief, your conversation partner may think you are not as interesting or intelligent as you may be.

Use Quiet Pizzazz

You have to be interesting to the person you are talking to. You don't need to feign charisma—but have some pizzazz. Too much charisma may turn a person off.

Stay On-Track

While you are chatting away with a prospective mate, remember to find out the personal information that you need. Ask all the questions in a conversational tone of voice. Be casual and friendly, but steer the discussion in directions that you want answers to.

Make the Person Feel Good

Compliment the candidate about things you truly like. Demonstrate to the person, in an appropriate way, that you respect and think highly of him or her.

Project Some Feeling

When you are talking with a new prospect you like, encourage some warmth to be felt through your conversation and body language. Since new acquaintances are usually a little uncomfortable at first, your ability to project warm feelings will make them more responsive sooner.

Dispel Anxiety

When a person who attracts you does make contact, he or she may not be very poised. Don't dismiss the person as overly inhibited. He or she may be having fears of being rejected. Dispel the anxiety with a little humor and respect the person for taking the initiative.

Start Off Right

If you are a little nervous, remain positive and continue talking. Feign confidence until you begin to feel it. The other person may not notice how nervous you are or any minor slip-ups you may have made. In fact, any minor *faux pas* will make you seem all the more human and may serve to reassure your prospective mate.

Flirt a Little

Show your attraction to the other person by flirtatious body language, as well as friendly conversation. You can be modest and quite subtle, but still effectively get your message across. The moment you spot someone who interests you, begin looking into the person's eyes. Watch for the appropriate reaction and act accordingly. If it goes nowhere, just move on. It may be that the person doesn't know how to flirt without a scorecard. Others who flirt with you may be "all show and no go." Just move on. They may be compulsive flirts who demand attention and then have nothing to offer you.

Body Language

Sixty-five percent of all communication is nonverbal. We are continually transmitting and receiving subtle signals. When you first spot someone, you notice the way that person stands, dresses, and eats. The impressions are positive, negative, or neutral.

When you develop good body-language skills, you can discern more from what a person does than from what he or she says.

Our behavior is not an accident. While we can turn a smile on or off, it is more difficult to control the way one stands or walks. Even when we act with greater deliberation, we often fall back into our comfortable, unrehearsed behavior patterns. For example, a false smile tends to slip away in a short time.

Compare the verbal messages you are receiving with the nonverbal behavior you are observing. The closer the two match, the surer you can be of that person's integrity. If someone is telling you how sincere he or she is while looking you directly in the eyes and leaning forward, you have good grounds to believe that person. If, on the other hand, the person's arms are crossed and he or she is unwilling to look you in the eye, the "message" is that your prospect is not truly open to involvement.

During first encounters with a new person, you don't know this individual's love history, life experiences, or other information. You have to observe and rely on whatever messages his or her body positioning or movements are sending. People tell us only what they want us to know, but their body language generally doesn't lie.

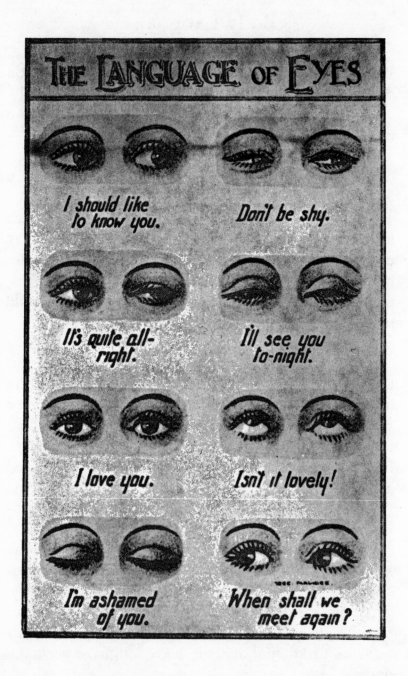

The more complex or secretive the person, the more you need to concentrate on his or her body language. When you know what someone is thinking, you can react in a way that maximizes the probability of getting what you want. You will suffer less rejection, be more confident, and appear more attractive to others.

Understanding body language cuts down the time needed to make the correct judgment. Early insights reduce disappointments, such as getting stuck with the wrong person or having your advances rebuffed.

Are You Flirting Enough?

Flirting or playing at love can create the environment for romantic interest to take place. Some people believe that flirting is unnecessary, but the more you appreciate the purpose of flirting and its benefits, the more you will make every effort to become good at it. The better a flirt you are, the more relaxed you will be with the opposite sex. Flirting allows potential marriage partners to know that you exist. The key to successful flirting is the correct use and interpretation of body language.

Women Need to Flirt

Recent research shows that women's flirtatious behavior gets men to act. Without it, little will happen. Flirting allows women to check out a man's interest without being too direct. Psychologist Monica Moore studied women at a singles bar and found that the most common nonverbal ways women flirt are smiling, moving with the music, laughing, using quick darting glances, touching their hair and leaning closer toward the man of their interest.

How to Get a Fix on Someone

Reading someone is both an art and a science. The key is to look the person over from head to toe. Notice the person's eyes, face, hair, clothes, stance, voice, handshake, and how far he or she stands from you.

You must make an assessment based on all of the available information. The key is to look carefully at every aspect of the person and watch for consistency. As you talk, see if the body language changes and in what ways.

The more open gestures you observe, the more interested the person is. Notice if your prospect's jacket is open, if his arms and legs are spread or folded, if she smiles and laughs easily, and if those facial muscles are tense or relaxed. When people are romantically interested their eyes blink faster, they maintain eye contact longer, and they subconsciously match your own gestures—smiling and laughing when you do.

When someone lacks interest in you, it is expressed through body language as well. For instance, you may be getting the proverbial cold shoulder from someone. There is a strong likelihood that this person doesn't care for you. You should cut your losses and politely move on. It is extremely helpful to watch for negative body-language signals because people often find it difficult or impossible to verbalize that a person is not for them.

6

ॐ

It Begins With Hello. . .

"Your conversation only
has to be good enough
for the person you are
talking to."

— Dr. Gallatin

119

Getting It Going

This chapter will show you:
- How to open and close conversations.
- How to enhance your conversational skills.
- How to approach someone who's already busy chatting.
- How to follow the six steps of a conversation.

When we ask a stranger for information, that is often all we get. Give that interesting stranger a reason to expand a response into a conversation. For example, you may be sitting on a park bench and someone with a newspaper sits down within meeting distance. You might say, "Hi! Could I take a look at the business section for a minute?" Look briefly then make a comment ("The market is up."). Follow up with a question ("Do you play the market yourself?"). The answer — whether it is "Yes" or "No" — will allow for further discussion or another question. The more natural, the better.

If properly handled, most people will talk longer than you think and will appreciate your attention. Few interested singles will push you away and the conversation can continue. Marriage will be your ultimate reward.

A woman who asks for the sports section, in the situation above, is sure to win a conversation — if not a date for the big game against the Dodgers, Knicks, or Bears. What you need are questions and responses that fit naturally in the situation, that are emotionally and politically neutral, and that allow the person to comfortably respond and continue talking.

The Moment of Truth

We often go around wanting to meet the right person. We dress well, check ourselves in mirrors or store windows, and then, when social opportunities arise, don't always respond quickly enough—or at all. It's not prepared lines that are needed, but the state of mind to say the appropriate thing at any given time.

Your Attitude

A conversation that doesn't get you a phone number, date, or proposal of marriage is not a failed or wasted opportunity. At the very least you made waiting for that train more interesting. All conversations, no matter the length, prepare you for the next one. Make the most out of every conversation and you will always come out ahead.

How to Ask Him Comfortably

A woman may be with a man who interests her, but the request for her phone number is somehow never made. She can just give up, and leave—like most women —or she can help him out.

As a successful female, you should say to him, "I have enjoyed chatting with you, but I have to get going now." Look him squarely in the eyes. Hesitate for a moment. He should either say, "Why don't you give me your number?" or "It would be nice to talk again." You should then say, "Sure, I will be glad to exchange home phone numbers."

If he merely responds with a "Take care," you can quickly leave or you can say, "It would be nice to talk again." This leaves him with a stronger hint to ask for your number.

The last choice is to directly ask for his number by saying, "Why don't we exchange home phone numbers so we can contact each other?" If the answer is "No," forget you ever saw him. You can do better.

If you have already exchanged home phone numbers, say to him, "I look forward to your call." The ball is now in his court. If he calls, you are ahead. Make sure you have an answering machine and have a message that promises a return call. If he doesn't call, I wouldn't especially recommend calling him. The probabilities of his being interested are limited. He may be committed elsewhere and only took your number to be polite.

Here's a number to give out. If you are at a party or a bar, approach someone who interests you and write down 07734. Ask the person if he or she knows what it means. When you hear the "No," tell the person to turn the number upside down. It spells the word HELLO. You've earned a smile and your conversation has begun!

A little artificial? Okay, but sometimes a prepared ice-breaker comes in handy.

What's a Person Like You Doing with a Line Like This?

We shouldn't have to use opening lines like "Do you come here often?" When push comes to shove, however, you might resort to them.

When we are nervous we use opening lines to get a conversation going without having to think.

Practically every woman I have interviewed felt that such lines were a distinct turn-off. Some women did understand, however, that stock phrases allow the more inhibited men to approach.

The rule is: Don't use a line if you can avoid it. Lines make your intentions too obvious, especially if you approach someone in a natural setting like a bank. Not using a line where it is expected (for example, in a bar) will get you more favorable attention.

Purposeful Listening

It is easy to underestimate the importance of careful listening. In order to have good interaction and real involvement, you have to discover a person's needs, feelings, and beliefs

Listening requires more than keeping quiet while someone is talking. J. C. Penney, the founder of the department store, said: "For most of us, listening, whether in a social conversation or around the table at a conference, is just a pause we feel obligated to grant a speaker until we again have a chance to air our opinion."

Listen for intent, not just for the facts. What seems to matter most to her? What subjects does he bring up? How does she respond to your suggestions? Is he interested in anything besides his dog and running? Purposeful listening forces you to focus on the other person, not on yourself. Too often, we don't hear the person out. Be patient; it takes most people a few minutes to warm up. Careful listening will also help you identify any problems with that romantic prospect.

Getting Past the Opener

If someone interesting approaches you and says, "The doughnuts are stale," you don't have to get locked into a five-minute discussion about stale doughnuts. Say something like "Thanks for the warning. Can I watch you eat for a while?" I want to see if you survive the rest of the refreshments. Opening lines are just that. When confronted with them, be sure to change the topic to one of your choosing. All the opening line is saying is, "May I talk with you?"

Opening Up

Most of us are hesitant to ask or answer what we consider to be personal questions from a stranger. "Personal" can range from what neighborhood someone lives in, to the year one graduated college, or to the amount of rent one pays.

You don't want to open with a personal question. It may put the person on edge and get him or her self-conscious about rejection. A guy who is asked about his profession right away might get defensive and feel he has to exaggerate to impress you.

How can you motivate a stranger to get personal? The more comfortable you make a person, the more he or she will tell you and the sooner. Women tend to be somewhat more guarded than men, because they have been brought up to be leery of men they don't know. A naturally flowing conversation will yield more personal data that you might think. The way to encourage personal conversation is to open up about yourself first. Act like it is perfectly natural to mention your former spouse, and you are likely to get the other person's marital status. You might want to casually drop the phrase "Your wife" or "Your husband" and see if the person corrects you.

When conversing with someone in a superior career situation, don't get defensive. If you are self-conscious about an unflattering job, don't say, "I am only a file clerk and hate my nowhere job." The negativism only aggravates your situation and identifies you as a nowhere person. If you have higher ambitions you could honestly and confidently say, "I'm studying to be a dietitian, but I'm presently doing office work."

Tips For Good Conversation

- Talk with and listen to good conversationalists.
- Read magazines, books, and newspapers to be up on current events and topics.
- Don't assume you have to be an expert to talk. You don't need an advanced degree in political science to express an opinion on the upcoming elections.

- On the other hand, don't fake knowledge or try to wing it when you don't know anything about a topic.
- Talk to as many people as possible, whenever possible, in order to get used to the idea of having a casual conversation.
- Don't think about being rejected.
- Express your opinion; don't be afraid to differ with someone.
- When lost for a topic of conversation, refer to the immediate setting or situation.
- Act confident.
- End most of your remarks with a question that will help maintain the conversation.
- Don't touch a stranger during a first conversation.
- Relax and have a good conversation; don't try to make it the world's most profound or meaningful dialogue.

A Poor Conversationalist:

- Opens with a negative comment like "The service here is horrible; I'll never come back."
- Speaks so fast that the listener cannot pay serious attention.
- Speaks so slowly that the listener must have the patience of a saint.
- Is too intense, scaring the listener with unduly serious topics.
- Asks very personal questions too directly and too soon.
- Makes the conversation sound like an interview.
- Never pauses.
- Answers a simple question with a tedious monologue or excessive examples.

- Focuses too much on himself or herself.
- Doesn't talk enough or prompt the other person.

Starters

Make it easy for another to start talking to you. Try one of the following conversation starters.

- Carry a current best-selling book.
- Wear an appropriate but eye-catching outfit.
- Carry an interesting shopping bag or a company briefcase.
- Walk an unsual dog.
- Sit one seat away from someone who interests you.
- Wear some sports paraphernalia of your local team.

Excuse Me

We often spot someone interesting who is busy talking with friends or acquaintances. Should we just shrug our shoulders and walk away or try to do something about it? If handled properly, you won't have to feel that you are doing something inappropriate.

If two men or women are casually talking at a party, in a bar, or even on a park bench, it doesn't mean that one or both of them would also not be interested in talking to someone they find attractive. Especially in social settings they may be talking to each other to avoid feeling self-conscious. They may have gotten tired of waiting for Mr. or Miss "Right" to come over.

Now that you don't feel you're interrupting something important, don't feel guilty about singling out the one you are especially interested in.

Walk over and stand four feet or so from the two people talking. Look (don't stare) directly at the one you want to speak with. When he or she notices you, smile slightly. If the two are in an intense conversation, you should gracefully slip away for a while.

This is not the right time. Otherwise, listen and catch the drift of their conversation. Seek an opening where you can say something appropriate. When you make that comment, look directly at the person you want to meet. If you are not dealt into the conversation, the apple of your eye may either not be interested in you or may not know what to do. Casually move back a few feet, but keep your eyes open to see if they separate. If they do, walk over, act like nothing happened, and begin again. This approach may not always work, but it only has to work once.

When you start talking with the one that you are particularly interested in, let the other person in on the conversation so she doesn't feel completely left out. Just make your preference clear while you converse. In a few minutes, the other person should get the message and move away. If her friend doesn't leave, focus on the person you are interested in and say, I see I have caught you while you are busy. I have to go now, but I would like to exchange phone numbers and give you a call. We can talk later, OK?" Pull out your pen and card; don't wait for permission.

Getting Unstuck

Getting a spontaneous conversation started, maintaining it, and ending it comfortably for both parties is an art as well as a science. Almost everyone at times seems to get stuck somewhere along the way.

I have carefully analyzed hundreds of conversations and broken them down into six steps. By understanding the dynamics of each of the six steps, you will talk more smoothly and get bogged down less often. This section will help you fully appreciate the conversational process that each of you is going through. You will be able to help your new friend over any hurdles, if necessary. You will both end up winners.

The Six Steps of a Conversation

Step One: The Opening

Here is where you get the ball rolling. You don't have to do anything spectacular, but you have to "break the ice." As Miss Manners (Judith Martin) says, "This is one time where bland is better." Men or women can use the natural openers that have proven themselves at singles activities as well as in everyday life. For example: "Hi, which panelist did you find the most interesting?" You could always fall back on, "Could you tell me the time?" Why take a chance that you may be coming on too strong? Be friendly, smile when appropriate, make a comment, and follow it up with a question. For example: "Hi, where did you get those incredible boots?" or "Which wine would you recommend?" Make the next step easy for even the most timid.

It is easy to overdo the "opening." It is wrong to assume that you have to immediately charm the pants off that interesting stranger. Assume there is a fair chance the person is interested, but enter your prospect's world as gently as possible.

Where you meet makes a difference. At a party you are psyched up and prepared, but at the supermarket you may be concerned about the next item on your shopping list. Meeting naturally in the course of your everyday life requires somewhat better techniques and more understanding of body language and human nature; in either case you have to begin with some kind of opening.

Step Two: The Comeback

The opening is followed up by the "comeback." Respond right away, in a friendly manner, with an answer and a follow-up question that do not break the momentum. If someone says, "Hi, what did you think of the speaker?", say "I liked what he said about...." Then ask, "What did you think of...?" If the speaker wasn't great, focus on something positive and valuable, even if it was one small point. Even when giving the time, come back with, "Do you know when the store closes?" if you want to keep the ball rolling. Encourage the conversation by being casual and unassuming.

Don't count on a particular response from anyone. Be prepared to continue the conversation even if you get a minimal reaction. It may be the person is very interested but needs a minute to catch his or her breath. Don't be put off by an overused line or a little nervousness. The person may not be as skilled at talking to strangers as you are. What is most important is that you are interested and you are trying to find a common ground to continue your new friendship.

It is best not to take the other person's interest for granted. Initial friendliness may not necessarily be a sign of any special attraction. Singles can be very skeptical, so your conversation should display sincere interest if you want to successfully make your feelings known.

Step Three: The Starting Topic

Whether you begin discussing the wine and cheese or the speaker, you are on your way. Now you both have indicated some interest, you are speaking together comfortably and are ready to assess your romantic potential. You are still in the small-talk stage, however. The starting topic gives you something deeper to hook into. The successful starting topic allows you both to have something to say and gives you both an opportunity to create a good impression. The conversation doesn't have to be earthshaking, but both parties should actively help to keep it going. The amount of involvement doesn't have to be equal; women often talk less than men at this stage. What is important is that the involvement should be genuine.

If the conversation begins at stage three, remember that your prospect may need some warm-up time.

Don't allow yourself to get bogged down in the details. You are looking for attitudes, general impressions, and overall interest. Your partner's omissions may be just as important as what is said. Usually within minutes the conversation reaches a lull, and both parties become quiet. Unless something happens quickly, it can be finished before it has had a chance to develop.

Step Four: The Lull/Transition

After you have discussed the starting topic, a lull often develops and many conversations end here after a minute or two of awkward and forced communication. If you and the other person don't want to continue, that is one thing, but a good conversation that dies young is an avoidable tragedy. Based on what you have learned from the person so far or from the situation you find yourself in, pick a topic that you could both easily talk about for several more minutes. Hobbies or travel provide fertile and natural areas to express oneself.

If you had been discussing the wine and cheese in drawn-out detail, simply say when the discussion fades out, "Summer is almost here; are you planning to take a vacation?" or "Are you going anywhere special over Christmas?" Even if the answer is "I don't plan to take a vacation," you can ask where the person goes when he or she can take time off. If there are professional reasons why the person cannot take an extended vacation, you might discuss them instead.

You get the idea. If the person is interested, there should be little resistance. He or she will be glad that you've broadened the conversation. Both of you have a chance to see if your initial interest was justified and if there's a real chance of progressing to an exchange of phone numbers.

Step Five: The Major Topic

The transition has provided you with a back-up topic to further explore your new discovery. What interests does the person have? What does the person do for a living? Where was he or she raised? Important biographical events, major beliefs and values, religion, etc., should all emerge if the two of you are rubbing antennae.

Was the person ever married? Any children? If yes, how old are they? If your partner has never married, see if you can find out why not. Educational and professional inquiries are especially common and natural for those still in school.

Your conversation should flow smoothly. Make sure to express your opinion. Show the person who you are and how you feel. If the person is not interested in you, it is better to know sooner rather than later. With the right person and the right topic, the time should fly by. The "major topic," then, is yourselves. Don't flit from one topic to another but do talk about more than one subject. Don't "interview" your prospect with a one-sided inquest in place of a dialogue.

Step Six: The Ending/Farewell

The final step is to take specific action, either by disengaging, leaving, or exchanging phone numbers. You could ask for the number in as early as ten minutes into the conversation, especially if circumstances are pressing. In most cases, you shouldn't appear too anxious. A woman has to feel that you know enough about her, or she may dismiss you as a number collector. Make sure your mind agrees with your eye. Too quick a judgment may turn out to be a mistake. Once you get the number, you can continue the conversation for as long as you both want to or as long as you are able to. You don't have to leave immediately, although a good performer leaves the audience begging for more. You may want to maintain some excitement, so your call will be greatly anticipated.

It is advisable to get a phone number even though

you could go on talking longer. An interested woman is anticipating such a request. After you get her number and don't leave immediately, you've reassured her of your sincerity. She is then more likely to let her guard down, and you will be able to find out additional information. As you learn about her feelings and experiences you will be able to decide how soon to call her and how to best date her. If appropriate, you can suggest going to an event or performance right then and there.

Ask for the phone number in a straightforward manner. Look the person in the eyes and say, "Mary, I enjoyed talking with you and would like very much to exchange home phone numbers." If you've quickly developed a rapport, add something definite: "I would like to exchange home phone numbers with you and take you out to dinner." Without hesitating, offer your business card or personal card and ask for her home number.

If the woman is doing the asking, she may suggest meeting or eating somewhere that is mutually convenient. She may ask for a man's phone number under the guise of seeking professional advice or drawing upon his expertise in some area. If a fellow hesitates to give you his home number it might mean there's a woman at home that he'd rather you didn't know about.

Yes, I Can't

It may take you a while to learn how to say "No" comfortably and politely. It is better to say "No" now and not hurt someone more, later. You may not want to be so direct as to say, "I don't want to go out with you,

you are not my type." You might say, instead, "I appreciate the offer, but I have to decline. Take care."

If the person isn't right for you, or the timing is not appropriate, you are only hurting yourself by letting a conversation turn into a date.

The world from which you could choose a mate is not always as large as you want, so try not to insult someone you don't want to date. That same person could invite you to a party or know someone who could be good for you.

Pest Control

To discourage someone from talking with you, just reverse some of the guidelines above. Be negative. Bring up controversial subjects. Be painfully honest and un-diplomatic. Minimize eye contact and look around a lot. Step back a little more than is customary. Get overly serious and don't smile. Say just enough to not be rude. Give shorter and shorter responses.

If the person who approached you is used to being rejected, is particularly fond of you, is insensitive, or feels that you are playing hard-to-get, he or she may not be easily put off. Your best bet is to be direct. For example: "Bob, I appreciate your interest, but I don't feel the same way." If he persists you simply say, "There is nothing more to discuss. Take care." Don't let anyone pressure you, and don't feel guilty for not playing social worker to the local losers.

You don't have to excuse yourself to go to the ladies' room or to make a phone call. Such excuses may make it harder on you to comfortably move around. If you turn someone down firmly but nicely, you don't have to feel awkward if you bump into him or her later at the party or in the near future.

A "No" Need Not End a Conversation

If you have just begun talking to someone and get a "No" when you ask, "Have you ever been here before?"—that doesn't mean the person doesn't want to talk to you. It could just mean that he or she is very honest. What you want to do is to ask another question. Avoid a "No" by presenting a choice: "Which tie do you like best, this one or this one?"

An Example of Not Saying "No"

Bob met a woman while having lunch in a local eatery. They were soon in an animated discussion. When her time was up, she said she had to leave but she appeared to be hesitating. Bob asked for her number. He called her the next day and left a message on her telephone answering machine, saying he would call the next evening. He called again, got the machine and left another message. He didn't receive a return call. Bob finally wrote her off and went about his life. A short time afterward, Bob was sitting in the same local eatery, and in walked the same woman on the arm of a man. She would have made it easier for both of them if she had declined to give her number in the first place.

Ralph, How About Friday Night?

Increasingly, today's men are being put in the position of having to say "Yes" or "No" to a woman's question. A man admires a woman for asking, but if she is not his type he should simply say, "I appreciate your interest but I cannot." The less you say, the better. Unlike some boorish men, the female of the species will rarely press on when they hear a "No." Be kind and gentle to minimize the discomfort. You want her to feel free to talk to you again, or vice versa. You may end up seeing her again at other social functions or being introduced to her roommate. The world is smaller than you think.

Since saying "No" can be so difficult, you may have to decide how you are going to go about it. The best way is to prepare some strategies to use when you need them.

Why Men Don't Ask

There are many reasons why a man might not ask for your number after a pleasant conversation of some length. He may not be that interested romantically, even though he enjoyed talking with you. He may not be sure what to do. He might not be available. He could be smitten with you but knows he cannot get involved.

Perhaps he felt you didn't like him enough. No man or woman should let ten minutes of a lively conversation go by without telegraphing real interest to the partner. Beyond the body language already discussed, slip in a compliment or two if you really want him to ask for your last name and number.

7

Beating Rejection

**"Don't make rejection
your silent partner."**

— Dr. Gallatin

Reject Rejection

The fear of not getting a positive response is a major reason singles don't meet more potential partners and get married sooner. The more you go out, the more rejection you face. Every rejection makes it harder to begin again. The longer we wait between encounters, the more difficult it is to get moving again. While we know that a particular rejection shouldn't hold us back and that it is not the end of the world, it still gets to us and often slows us down. Learning to take rejection in stride can make it possible for you to comfortably approach any attractive individual at any time. Rejecting rejection will make your life as a single less traumatic and more enjoyable.

"Who's Next"

Just how do you get philosophical about rejection when it is so intensely personal? You have to realize that not everyone will be interested in you, for a variety of reasons. If the person is not interested, no matter how hurt you feel, you must realize that the longer you postpone re-entering the social environment the more you are wasting valuable time feeling sorry for yourself. Look forward to meeting the next person instead of dwelling on the disappointment of the last one. When you think about who's next, you are going in the right direction. The very next person you meet could be your life partner. Concentrate on the excitement of that prospect and get back out there.

You Haven't Been Totally Rejected

You have been rejected when a particular person is not interested in you as a prospective marriage partner. This doesn't mean that this person doesn't like many things about you. The prospect doesn't see you as marriage material. You like many people that you wouldn't go ahead and marry. Be grateful that you were turned down rather than played with for a few months.

Don't Be Beaten Before You Start

If you anticipate rejection, you will find it hard to get up the nerve or the energy to do your best. The fear of rejection can be picked up by others, and this may destroy any opportunity you have of being successful.

Don't play the martyr and wear rejection like a badge. You won't get too far by campaigning for people's sympathy. Think in terms of acceptance, not rejection. If you have been rejected by ten people in a row and the eleventh wants to go out with you, the ten who weren't interested in you shouldn't matter at all.

Home Run Hitters Strike Out Most

If you are rejected often, you may come to feel that you are a loser. You will only be a loser if you don't continue to risk losing in that quest for the one victory you need. People forget that winners are actually rejected more than losers because they take more chances, making themselves more available to a wider variety of romantic prospects. Look at it in baseball terms. The big home run hitters strike out most. They don't always get a lot of hits and their batting averages are often low. You're going for the fences. You are going to round the bases and come home.

Consequences of the Fear of Rejection

If you are consciously or unconsciously doing everything in your power to avoid the possibility of rejection, you will pay the price in the following ways:

- You will approach fewer new people.
- You will lower your standards, seeking romantic prospects among less desirable people.
- You will expect—and get—less from dates.
- You will need more healing time between relationships.

To find the best person for you, you may have to approach and date many people before discovering someone you like who returns your interest. The more you are able to accept rejection, the less the process will bother you. If the fear of rejection is too overwhelming, you will see more candidates through rose-colored glasses. Men will approach only those women they believe will not turn them down. Women who are overly concerned with the possibility of rejection will not directly or indirectly approach men. Insecurity is a hindrance to beauty that no cosmetic can cover up.

If rejection makes you lower your expectations, you will be setting yourself up for a greater disappointment in the long run. Once you get emotionally involved with someone who is not really what you want, it is harder to break away. Marry someone who could never forget you, but don't marry someone because he or she will never reject you.

Attractive, successful people have many more social opportunities and can afford to be the most selective. They are in a position to do a lot of the rejecting. You are better off being rejected by the more selective prospects who interest you, rather than settling for someone less than you feel you deserve. If you are persistent it will only be a matter of time before one of them will want to love, cherish, and marry you. Since every social contact can lead to rejection, you may hesitate too often when an opportunity for natural meeting arises. That bus ride or bank line lasts only a few minutes. Don't let fear of rejection make you miss that precious window of opportunity.

Drawing by Mort Gerberg; © 1982 The New Yorker Magazine, Inc.

Rejection's Family Ties

When we are rejected, we recall past rejections by parents, siblings or former lovers. Try to consciously dissociate heavy earlier experiences from that "No" by people you barely know. Rejection bothers us because of our need for love and approval. Remember that the person who declines to go out with you on a first or a second date is not declaring you unworthy of love. Have patience.

Total Acceptance

Trying to win over every prospective mate is both tiring and futile. What you should do is give yourself a chance with each person. We have been raised to be overly concerned with other people's opinions of us, even perfect strangers. Each time we fail, we make ourselves miserable. What happened to Bill illustrates how this self-defeating attitude gets in our way. Bill went to Adam's Apple in New York City, ordered a drink, and soon spotted a woman who interested him at the other end of the bar. He gulped down a scotch to strengthen his resolve for his long journey around the bar. He felt the eyes of everyone on him as he approached her. After a few minutes, she excused herself and left to go to the ladies' room. She didn't return. He quickly and self-consciously returned to his former bar stool, while gulping down another scotch. Red-faced and perspiring, Bill escaped the scene of his rejection. It was only 10:30 P.M. He wondered if he should try another place down the block. Instead, he drove home. The idea of further humiliation was too disturbing.

What really happened back at Adam's Apple, where no one knew Bill or cared about his "failure?" The woman who turned him down was getting a divorce and wasn't ready to get involved with anyone at this time. Bill hadn't failed at all. Ms. Blonde simply was not available. But Bill felt that he had struck out in front of a national audience. Bill's fear of public disapproval was more important than the facts.

All Rejection Is Not the Same

Bill's failure was no rejection. There are two categories of rejection: personal and circumstantial. Understanding the difference between these two types will give you a clearer perspective and help you to better accept the rejections you will encounter.

Personal Rejection

When a romantic prospect turns you down because of your weight, looks, personality, or the way you talk— then you have been rejected personally. These rejections, based on externals, can be reduced with some effort on your part. You can improve your accent or diction, get that corrective surgery, or go on that diet.

Circumstantial Rejection

Much rejection you will encounter is actually beyond your control. Like Bill, you may be turned away for reasons that have nothing directly to do with you. The person you are talking with may be married, living with someone, or otherwise not ready to date. This person may not choose to tell you why he or she is not available. Think positively and assume that most of your rejections are circumstantial and that, in other instances, the person would be happy to go out with you. Circumstantial rejection occurs when you have no realistic chance of being seriously considered. If you were rejected because of your height, race, or religion, try to see it as a circumstantial rejection and not a personal one.

You May Need More Rejection

If you are not meeting enough good candidates, you are probably playing it too safe—dating people that are not challenging enough or appropriate for you. This approach only adds to the time it will take to meet your ideal mate.

You may also be spending too much time analyzing and recovering from each rejection. The way to resolve these situations is to go out more often and give yourself enough opportunities to be rejected. Let your rejections serve to toughen you a bit. Get your skin just callous enough so that you don't raise a blister every time you swing that racket.

Sooner Is Better Than Later

When you are out there actively seeking a mate, you can be rejected at any point. Most of us are particularly concerned about being initially rejected, when this should be the least troubling of all. You shouldn't feel broken-hearted after talking to a stranger for ten minutes. Let's review the major rejection periods:

A KNIFE, YOUR PHONE NUMBER, A NAPKIN, AND THE SALT?

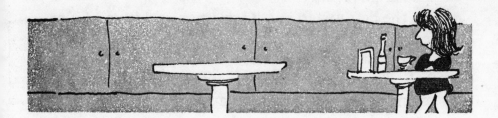

Immediate Rejection

The fear of being rejected right away keeps both men and women from approaching and making a confident, positive first impression. More women would approach men today if rejection didn't hold them back. While women often say it is their upbringing that prevents them from approaching an attractive man, it is more likely their fear of being publicly turned down. Immediate rejection is uncomfortable because it usually takes place within touching distance of someone we have just met. You must consciously minimize the effects of immediate rejection from a stranger since you've invested little time and even less emotion.

Rejection After a Few Dates

Being rejected after a few dates can be painful. Your new friend has gotten to know something about you, and therefore the rejection is based on more than a superficial impression. Some feelings may have begun to develop. At this point, it is harder to rationalize that he or she doesn't really know you. While the person may not know your life history, he or she rules you out as spouse material.

The best way to handle rejection at this point is to realize that the shoe didn't fit, so he or she didn't wear it. Be pleased that you were worthy of a long, serious look. Even though you were interested in that person, you must get busy finding someone else who would be interested in you. You know that you have a lot going for you, so it should not take too long before you meet someone new who would like to become more seriously involved with you.

On the first few dates, it is best to concentrate your energy on getting to know the person. Don't let your imagination run wild and begin planning your wedding.

Rejection After Sex

Whether it is the first or the fourth date, it can be pretty rough emotionally if someone you decided to have sex with goes ahead and "dumps" you. You can feel abused and used. You may regret going too far too fast.

When you sleep with someone you don't know well, you are taking a certain risk that the kissing, closeness and "sweet nothings" whispered in your ear at just the right time were merely calculating, insincere expressions of the moment. Less experienced daters discover that "sweet nothings" are usually just that when uttered in bed. For too many men, "I love you" is merely a long ejaculation.

If you decide to have sex with someone you don't know very well, make sure you get out of it what you need and realize in advance that you are taking a chance. If you are likely to link sexual feelings with strong emotional attachment, then you are much better off postponing sexual activity.

Men especially will tend to brood on their "performance," suffering wounds to the libido as well as to the heart when a sexual relationship ends in rejection.

Take away something positive from the affair. At least the opposite sex finds you sexually attractive. You have the physical charms to entice somebody new, so get out there—but reassess the timing of your sexual involvement.

Rejection After
You Become Involved

Once you become intensely involved with someone, regardless of the reason, it is going to take you a while to recover from rejection. The question is how long? The sooner the healing takes place, the better off you will be. Being upset for a short period of time is healthy and normal. A long period of mourning can be dangerous; you may fall into self-destructive patterns that will jeopardize future involvements.

Circle a date on your calendar a few weeks ahead and promise yourself that you will go out that night. You are sadder but wiser. You know that you have what it takes to sustain a serious relationship. You are ahead of the game. Your next involvement, it is hoped, will be forever.

You Have to Be Accepted Before
You Can Be Rejected

You may feel rejected when you were never actually accepted in the first place. For example, if you are at a party and a prospect starts talking with you, this doesn't mean that his or her interest is genuine. It might simply mean that the person finds you conveniently available and doesn't want to stand alone looking unassertive or unpopular. A man or woman may respond to your advance simply to be polite. You can become a conversation piece, not the subject of serious scrutiny. Therefore you shouldn't feel rejected when a prospect disappears without a trace. If a woman agrees to go out with you, she might only be seeking an escort to a movie or a play, but not a serious date. Likewise, a man may ask a woman out to impress someone or gain entrance to a "couples only" event. In either case it is unproductive to waste valuable time feeling rejected. Simply move on and find someone better for you.

Reducing Your Chances of Being Rejected

The amount of rejection you will suffer depends in part on where you are meeting potential candidates. At commercial single events and bars, you should expect a higher rejection rate. The stress levels at these places are more intense because of the constant pressures to meet someone. The rule is that the more socially undesirable the participants see the setting, the greater the rejection rate. Participants at these events are rarely comfortable and usually will not be themselves.

Pressures also exist at dating and introduction services. But because an attempt is made to match you with a compatible person, your chances of early rejection are reduced.

Rejected Again

Don't run away. The first thing you should do is catch your breath. You will need a little time to analyze what happened. This may take thirty seconds or half an hour. Analyze the style of the person as well as the reasons for your rebuff. While poor style can be maddening, the reasons given are important to examine. Style is reflective of the other person; the reasons given may help you reduce the probability of future rejections.

8

*Enjoying Safe Sex
When You Are Ready*

"Find the right person,
then have a compassion
explosion."

— Dr. Gallatin

The Sex Factor

Behavioral scientists tell us that the average person often thinks about sex. Singles have more excuses for this natural preoccupation. While you are seeking a mate and courting, you are going to have to come to terms with your own and your date's sexual drives and desires. Many who would like to enjoy a regular sex life are inhibited by moral considerations and fear of sexually transmitted diseases. Very real issues, indeed. But on matters like these, consult your minister, priest, rabbi, therapist, or physician. This book does not advise on moral or medical issues. However, practice and follow the guidelines set forth in this book and premarital anything won't remain much of an issue.

And remember, following these guidelines is like making love: after a little experience you'll think you're an expert.

Recent Gallup polls establish that a majority of Americans approve of premarital sex.

Our sexual freedom and lack of guidelines put pressure on singles to have sex as long as there is some commitment and some available birth control. Today, each person and couple decide what is appropriate behavior.

Many singles are seeking a better sex life. Singles who are not involved in a stable relationship are generally wanting. They spend a lot of time looking for romance and sex, or try to busy themselves with other things so they won't have to think about their disappointing sex lives. This dissatisfaction and lack of peace can disrupt one's entire life, especially if one has a strong-sex-drive.

Sexual Compatability

Our inborn sex drives affect our compatability with others. There are three basic types of sex drives.

High

One who needs sex on at least a daily basis is a high-sex-drive person. This person will be sexually compatible only with another high-sex-drive person. Going out with a low-sex-drive person will create tension

because the high sex person will feel deprived while the low-sex-drive person will feel imposed upon.

Medium

A person with a medium sex drive has a need for regular sex, but there is room for negotiation. Such a person can adjust to living with the high- or the low-sex-drive person.

Low

A low-sex-drive person has minimal needs. Once a week may be too often. Sex is seen as more of an annoyance than anything else. The best match for a such a person is another low-sex-drive person or a medium-sex-drive person who cares enough to compromise.

Sexual Compatability Isn't Love

Finding the right partner doesn't mean automatic sexual bliss. You may discover that there are considerable differences in your preferences or in the amount of sex you each desire. The sooner you know if there are any real potential problems, the better. Couples counseling is available for the not-yet-married.

79 Positions

There is no shortage of books exploring and explaining sexual practices and techniques. My purpose is to help you find your ideal mate as quickly as possible so you can have fun learning with each other and using any tips you have picked up over time. Knowing 79 different positions to make love but not having the right partner to enjoy it with will lead to frustration, despair, anger, óne-night stands, and involvements with the wrong people.

Handling Advances

Many singles are hesitant to date because they are apprehensive about the demands for quick intimacy. Decide beforehand how you are going to handle any situation. You can be friendly and encouraging without compromising your principles. Work out an arrangement that you can both accept, remembering that too little sexual interest on the part of your boyfriend or girlfriend could signal a more serious problem down the road.

The most eligible or desirable people may not want to wait as long as you for the relationship to become sexual. Since it is easier for them to get dates, they may feel they have nothing to lose. This doesn't mean they are more capable of sensitivity and loving. You may be forced by this type of person to decide sooner in the relationship if investing your body is going to be worthwhile.

The One-Night Stand

Singles today are thinking more before going to bed with people they don't really know and probably will never see again. Women are more concerned about consequences than men, though casual sex has never stopped because of the fear of disease.

Casual sex is not always an accident for quite a few women. The major reason the average woman goes for a one-night stand is that she gets to the point where some touching, sweet words, and attention outweigh the risks. It becomes easier to accept if one has been out of a relationship for a while.

An occasional one-night stand is one thing, but if this type of encounter predominates, then you probably have serious problems in forming a relationship.

Do You Need Your Doorman's or Neighbors' Approval?

If you live in a building with a doorman or have nosy neighbors, you may feel self-conscious about bringing a date into your apartment.

While you may feel uncomfortable with the doorman announcing a different man every few days or opening the door for both of you, you know what you are doing and don't need to make any excuses to anyone.

Just because you invite a man over to relax, talk informally, and have dessert or a drink, it doesn't mean there is any hanky panky going on—no matter how late he stays. Conduct yourself in a ladylike manner. Your neighbors may not approve, but they will have precious little to discuss.

Should You or Shouldn't You?

While sex should be a result of your love or strong feelings for each other, often it is a spontaneous explosion of passion. Before going to bed with anyone, ask yourself the following questions:

- Is the person your type? If the person is not your type, you may wind up in the wrong relationship. The better the sex, the harder it may be to leave for a healthier relationship.
- Is this what you really want to do? Are you acting out of true desire or out of pressure?
- Will birth control be taken care of? Have the protection you need so you can relax and not worry about your lover's preparedness.
- If the person doesn't see you again, will you be able to accept it? Are you risking too much emotion or self-esteem on a relationship without a strong commitment? Think twice before dimming the lights in the future.

Love and Sex

Many women feel they should not become sexually involved with men they are not in love with. While going to bed with someone on a first or third meeting may be too soon, waiting three months may be a long time if you are seeing someone three times a week. It often takes a certain amount of adroitness to keep a good potential partner on hold without losing him.

A woman confided that she went out with Michael for six months, fell in love, and when they finally had sex, she found out why he wasn't in a hurry. He was impotent. She may not wait so long before finding out about the sexual ability of her next boyfriend.

If a man doesn't make enough sexual moves, it may not necessarily be a gentlemanly token of his esteem.

- He may not need you for sex.
- You may not be his ideal type of sex partner.
- He might be afraid he cannot please you.
- He could have a sexual dysfunction.

Saying "No"
With Your Foot in the Door

Even if you don't want to go to bed with someone at a particular time, you may still want to encourage him to continue seeing you. When a man stops asking—*that* is when your real problem with him begins. Learn how to say "No" so he will keep trying. If a man makes sexual advances the first time you talk to him or on the first date, it is easy to keep him waiting. Just say, "I would like to get to know you better. I have no particular time schedule. Things happen when the time is right and if they are meant to be." If he tries to stay over after a date, say the same thing. Remain good-natured, use your sense of humor, and stay relaxed. Tension indicates weakness.

The key to being successful and credible when saying "No" is to state your response in policy terms. For example, if a man you really don't know says, "Let's go back to my place and have some wine," you say, "It is not my policy to go to the apartment of a man I don't even know, regardless of how attractive I find him. I am sure a man like you can understand that. I would be glad to exchange home phone numbers with you so we can get to know each other better."

A sense of humor and good conversational skills are your best weapons. Suppose that on a first or second date a man drops you off at your home, you invite him in for a cup of coffee. If he then is in no hurry to leave, despite several hints, you should then say: "I enjoyed the evening and I am looking forward to seeing you again, but it is time to call it a night and leave." Stand up and move to the door. If he says he is exhausted and can barely move, act like you didn't hear what he said and respond, "I really had a good time going out with you, but now is not the time to have you spend the night. I enjoyed our date and hope you'll be calling me again real soon."

I Don't Usually, But . . .

If you decide to have sex with a man early on, you have to make it clear that you are making an exception because you are so attracted and you feel this relationship, while still in its early stages, is special. You can say at the appropriate time, "I normally wouldn't do this, but I feel very close to you." Don't say another word.

Many men don't respect a woman who goes to bed with them too soon. If you handle it with class and subtlety, he won't put you in a category with other women who casually sleep around. You have to know your man. Give the impression that your behavior is everything but casual.

What Turns Women On

There are four things that women look for in a man. The more of these you have, the greater your probability of attracting a better mate. The four are:

- Appearance—The better you look, the more women will be interested. You don't have to be tall, dark, and handsome, but a pot belly and sloppy clothes will reduce your chances.
- Confidence—A man who is confident will be seen as more powerful, more protective, and therefore more desirable.
- Attentiveness—It is hard to pay too much attention to a woman. She wants to know you care.
- Enthusiasm—A man who is full of life and vitality will do well. A woman won't picture you as her nightmare husband, spending weekends watching football games and guzzling beer.

If Your Body Is Not Perfect

Women are very conscious of their bodies and often feel there is some feature that is not attractive enough. If you don't like your body or some area of it, it becomes more difficult to project sex appeal. A scar on your stomach or a mark on your leg that you are self-conscious about doesn't mean you are undesirable. What is important is how you feel about yourself as a whole and how your partner feels about you.

An imperfection will be seen as unfortunate, but not a reason for you to be unsuccessful in finding a good mate. If your lover doesn't say anything, you should stop worrying about it or, when you get comfortable with him, say, "I hope this scar on my stomach doesn't turn you off." Wait for the answer. If he says it doesn't bother him and he is still dating you, forget all about it.

If you are not as physically attractive as you could be because you are too heavy, for example, and if you don't plan to lose weight, then you will have to pick a partner who will accept you as you are.

If your breasts are small and you are not hiding the fact, he probably likes women with small breasts or doesn't care about breast size. Men rarely go out regularly with women who do not fit their body type. Many women complain that their body is all that men care about. Most men, however, want more than one thing if a woman has more than one thing to offer. Single men and women both have to work on their worth and attractiveness while their clothes are still on.

If cosmetic surgery could correct some flaw, and you can afford it, perhaps you should consider it.

If you have had a mastectomy or other serious operation, this doesn't mean you have to give up hope of finding a mate. You will have to be better prepared, have inner strength, and realize that many men may not accept you—but you only need one good man to be happy.

If He Doesn't Act, You Can

If you want to get physical and your man doesn't—you can make a pass. You can help him without saying a word, and even allow him to appear to be the initiator. Look him in the eyes in a passionate way, dim the lights, put on the TV or slip a movie into your VCR, pour some wine, and sit within arm's reach. If need be, casually undo his tie or remove his jacket, telling him to relax, and how much you enjoy being with him. Don't worry that he may get the wrong impression. You are neither desperate nor lowering yourself, and he probably will be appreciative. You are simply providing your partner the opportunity to help you do what you and he want. He may hesitate because he is afraid of rejection and is unsure of what you want. Maybe in the past you have discouraged him too much. Few men will be put off if you make advances slowly, subtly, and in a non-demanding manner. Many men like or need a woman to come on to them.

Love or Obligation?

Do you see sex as an expression of love or as an obligation you cannot ignore if you want to capture and keep a mate? You don't owe anyone sex. Once you are in love, you may feel sex to be a mutual expression of your love. Fall in love with a good sexual partner. If you see sex as an obligation, then it will be more difficult to find a good mate. If you think men just want one thing, you will be consciously or unconsciously avoiding them or making excuses not to meet them.

9

Loving A Busy Professional

"Meet who you want,
leave the rest for
everyone else."
— Dr. Gallatin

167

Getting Started

It is disappointing to be a successful executive and not have the right mate to share one's life with.

Success in the business world doesn't bring success in one's personal life. Too often, a good business career comes at the expense of a good social life. You can, however, succeed both personally and professionally.

Business success may be easier to achieve because you can go to school and learn a specific trade. You can become an accountant or lawyer without investing a lot of emotional energy. In fact, getting emotional is often unproductive and unprofessional. A computer programmer need not to be a social butterfly to be a business success.

In the world of business, failure can easily be explained away by lack of sales support or saturation of the market.

The world of romance, however, requires you to constantly put yourself on the front line and to personally accept disappointment and rejection.

It is commonly believed that you cannot find both your ideal mate and build a successful career, particularly if you are a woman. Merely working nine-to-five probably won't get you up the corporate ladder. If you are an entrepreneur, you will more likely be working nine-to-nine. Finding love and marriage and pursuing wealth and fame too often seem to be mutually exclusive goals.

Fitting Love In

Dr. Sully Blotnick, in his book *Otherwise Engaged: The Private Lives of Successful Career Women*, says that women who had good careers but poor social lives suffer. He discovered that a good social life allows the career woman to unwind and relax from the stresses of the work world. He found that most women felt they had to choose between the two goals. Making this choice is costly and often leads to unhappiness.

Many women opted to curtail their personal lives and their search for a mate. A few women resolved the problem by selecting less educated or lower-income mates who would be financially dependent on them. Reliable house husbands are hard to find.

If you are putting in sixty- or eighty-hour weeks, it is hard to work romance into your schedule. Most men seem to find not having a special woman a serious problem and a major distraction. I know one woman who has a yearly income of more than a quarter of a million dollars—and no man in her life. Career success alone will bring happiness and personal fulfillment to precious few—but you can have your cake and eat it too. What I advocate is a balance between your career and personal pursuits.

No Time for Love

If you decide to focus most of your energy on developing your career, your personal life will suffer. You will:
• Become disgruntled.
• Pick poor partners.
• Stay too long in relationships that are going nowhere.

- Lack energy and excitement.
- Spend too much of your spare time seeking a mate.

Too Much Time for Love

You pay a price when you put too much of your energy into your social life. Some of the consequences include:

- Being less productive on the job.
- Not changing career or jobs when you should.
- Not asking for or getting the raises you deserve.

People Professions

Certain careers can actually help your social life because they are people-oriented and require the use and development of good social skills. Examples are sales, marketing, public relations, and education. Your line of work could provide many opportunities to meet a wide variety of people. If a salesman and teacher hook up, they may not have a six-figure combined income but they should have the social skills for a good marriage.

Business Success Alone Won't Get You Married

An Ivy League education, high social status, and a good salary don't necessarily mean that your social abilities are what they could be. Not everyone has a winning combination of looks, character, warmth, and success. Just because you are a successful executive doesn't mean that potential mates will be interested in you. Members of the opposite sex will not continue to date you simply because you are a business mogul. Good candidates will want you for yourself and because you are compatible.

The Best Jobs for Meeting Mates

Sitting by yourself or working in a small office will not help you meet a mate. While you may not want to accept a position for its social benefits, it could be an important consideration when you are out looking for a job.

Positions and occupations that offer visibility provide lots of people contact and can attract the type of person you are interested in. Some examples are provided to get you thinking:

- Sales positions with heavy client contact.
- Office situations with many people coming and going.
- Travel agencies.
- Airline Jobs.
- Financial consultant or advisory positions.
- Quality retail stores.
- Participating in trade shows, business seminars, conferences, and workshops.

Your job may provide you with more opportunities than you realize. If you meet interesting prospects who you will not be seeing again professionally, you can convert the situation to a social one. Properly handled, the potential date will not object to being approached and will be glad that you viewed his or her business card as a ticket to friendship—and did something about it.

Executive Sweet

Whether you would be happy with a busy or prominent executive or professional depends on your personality and life-style. If you want your mate home lavishing attention on you, then a doctor who has long hours and sleeps with a beeper may not be the answer. You might be better off with a freelancer who has a schedule you can more comfortably live with.

Get There First

At any particular time, relatively few desirable executives are available. Most are married, living with someone in a good relationship or otherwise not available.

Successful top executives have a lower divorce rate than less successful executives and the general public. When a successful executive does divorce, it is often to marry someone he or she had met before the official court proceedings are finalized. When he becomes widowed, as soon as he has decided to date again he will quickly find someone who will be only too glad to help put his life back together.

Therefore, if you want to marry a wealthy gentleman or lady executive, you may have to catch one on the way up.

Mixing Business With Pleasure

If an executive wants to meet new people for romantic purposes, he or she may go to a social activity attended by professionals or a networking party. Networking parties (or the art of making contacts) have taken on a magical quality. Executives come to meet each other, talk a few minutes, discuss business possibilities, and exchange business cards.

Special networking theme nights, featuring careers involving Wall Street, fashion, banking, acting, etc., help give the participants something in common to talk about. Soft recorded music plays in the background as guests circulate and attempt to make contacts. An outsider who just happens to drop in would get the feeling of being in a bar or lounge. The one difference is that the participants are given lapel holders to display their business cards as name badges.

One advantage to this method of meeting is that you don't have to be concerned with the topic of conversation. Your career is precisely what you are supposed to be discussing. Even if a person is not wearing a business card or a name tag with an occupation included, it is perfectly appropriate to ask someone what he or she does for a living.

From Business to Pleasure

While you may make some good business contacts, your real purpose is to make social contact. For example, if you are attending the monthly meeting of The American Society for Training and Development and have decided to use the cocktail hour before the formal program for social purposes, how can you do it in the most natural way possible? First of all, assume that many of the participants at the cocktail hour are there for the same purpose as you. Don't be one of those people who don't know how to switch from business to pleasure.

Approach whoever interests you and start the conversation as outlined in Chapter Six. Discuss business for five minutes or so to find out if there are any business possibilities. At the same time, try to send some verbal or nonverbal messages of personal interest.

There may be considerable interest but no hints or signals. If you want to elicit a response, simply say, "When you are not working overtime, what do you like to do for fun and relaxation?" Wait for the reply. If the answer is minimal or if the person switches back to business, say, "Why don't we talk again over the phone this week?" Say good-bye and move on to another possibility. You are not committing yourself to deal with this person; rather you are leaving yourself open for future contact if it is warranted.

You should expect a high rate of disappointment at business socials as preoccupation with business is often an excuse for not getting socially involved. Most of the

"We're in love."   *"Details at eleven."*

rejections you will experience here will be circumstantial, though, rather than personal. The average
person is not able to make the transition from a business
to a social mode. In other circumstances, that same
person might be more amenable.

Love in the Supply Room

Is meeting your marriage partner in the office appropriate? You might want to examine every possibility in
order to increase your chances of being married sooner.
Admittedly, an office romance is not for everyone. While
your office may not be a suitable place, other people's
offices may be promising. Reviewing this section might
help you see why others would try to meet you at work.

Business opportunities for meeting people outside
your own office include professional activities,
associations, conventions, and persons from other
companies—especially in your office building.

Romance in the workplace has undergone much
change. More women are executives. Women are no
longer taking low-level jobs in hopes of marrying the
boss. In addition, many executive women have adopted
the attitude of their male counterparts: that colleagues
shouldn't date in the office.

Let's say your firm hires someone who is just your
type, who is single and available, and who happens to
work on another floor and in a totally unrelated task.
You see the person in the company cafeteria and he or
she sits down next to you and starts a conversation. Why
should your colleague be off-limits when you are both
interested?

Advantages of Meeting in the Workplace

There are a number of distinct advantages in meeting in the workplace, including:

- You can really get to know someone well over a period of time.
- You can wait for the most auspicious and natural moments to indicate your interest.
- You can get important information about the person by utilizing the office's informal network.
- You minimize the risk of being rejected because you are not in a social setting.

Can You Handle an Office Romance?

It may not be wise for you to take advantage of a good opportunity at the office if you cannot handle some potential problems. In deciding whether an office romance is for you, ask yourself whether:

- You will be able to keep visible signs of affection— and more—out of the office.
- Your supervisors or colleagues would object.
- You will get hurt professionally.
- You can keep quiet until you announce your engagement.

The less successful your social life is away from the office, the more you should consider socializing where you work.

When an Office Romance Goes Sour

You both may feel uncomfortable and even vindictive, but sabotaging the other person can only harm you and your position. Talk to friends who will help you with the healing process. If your former partner bad-mouths you, the best policy is to ignore the person and move on.

The office is not a pick-up bar. You should use care when deciding whom to go out with and how involved to get. If you go through one person after another while at work, you will end up with a reputation that you deserve.

Working Women

Dr. Sully Blotnick in his 1958 study found that sixty-five percent of women between eighteen and thirty-five felt that taking a job was an opportunity to meet a mate. In his 1985 sample, however, Dr. Blotnick found that less than 6 percent felt work was a place to meet a mate.

How can we account for such a significant change in attitude? In 1958 women were looking for a husband first; and a job was merely the vehicle. Today's women are as interested in career growth and compensation as men are. Only if the right man comes along and if the conditions are appropriate is a career woman likely to get distracted by an attractive colleague.

All Businesses Are Not The Same

If you work in people businesses, such as advertising, sales, show biz, publishing, or the arts, meeting on the job is more acceptable. The more corporate businesses, such as banks, insurance companies, and brokerage firms, frown on dating clients or the person at the desk down the hall.

A person in one of these professions can meet people on the job by volunteering or getting a part-time job in the evening, on weekends, or on days off at a "people" place. These include health clubs, schools of adult education, career services organizations, or restaurants that cater to the people you would like to meet. Visibility in the right crowd is the key.

Having Lunch

If you bring your lunch or have it delivered to your desk, you are wasting an opportunity to socialize at a restaurant or employee lounge. While you sit alone and eat your food, gossip on the phone, or read the paper at your desk, you are passing up opportunities to meet a partner. You don't have to wait until after five to look for a mate.

Visit the shops, hangouts, and restaurants in your area where eligible men and women go. Most professionals eat at the same few places. When you have something to eat, take a look around before you sit down. If there is a potential partner close by, maneuver yourself to a seat next to or near that person. If you cannot meet the prospect this time, go back at the same time and try to spot him or her again. Your potential new friend will be flattered when you casually mention the food she was eating or the clothes he was wearing last Wednesday.

When a colleague you are not interested in asks you out and you don't want to go, say: "It is my policy not to date or get emotionally involved with anyone at work, regardless of how attracted I may be. I'm sure you can understand. But I appreciate your interest. Thanks for asking."

Then, excuse yourself and go back to work.

Always be courteous when you say "No." The other party was interested in knowing you; if you treat the person respectfully, you will minimize any bad feelings.

Lingering After Five

Unless you have dependents at home waiting for you, you don't have to run rush back to eat by yourself when the workday ends. Go to the health club in your business district or meet with friends. You can visit social spots near the office where attractive people go. Have a drink—soft or hard—talk to some potential dates, meet new friends. Why not go with someone from the office so you can encourage and support each other? Even if you do this once a week on Wednesday or Friday, you increase the probabilities of finding that marriageable executive.

People Meet and Date at Work Every Day

Harry and Leona Helmsley (the hotel king and queen) met on the job. A good friend of the mine found his wife at work. She was a few desks away. The whole office was at the ceremony. If you talk to others you will soon discover that meeting on the job is not as unheard of as many people believe.

Marrying Money

If you come from a wealthy background, it will be easier to marry into wealth. It is harder to marry money if you are not comfortable with the values and life-style that go with it. Just make sure that the person with money has other things you require in order for the relationship to last. It may take considerable effort and expense to land someone with wealth.

"Young, rich, and restless—that's a <u>career</u>?"

The best policy is not to focus all your energy and efforts on looking for someone who has money. If you are a woman, you have much greater chances of success if you are young, attractive, reasonably intelligent, and poised.

You should accept suitable dates who have the potential to make excellent mates. If your choice comes down to one with money and one with less money, you can choose the one with money.

You don't have to marry a kindhearted beggar, but you shouldn't blindly chase after the presidents of Fortune 500 companies. They may be successful, but they could also be selfish and unloving. Find someone who can support your preferred lifestyle, but don't marry someone who will be inclined to pull rank on you.

Don't Make Excuses

Executives with just as rigorous a schedule as yours do meet deadlines, develop good relationships, fall in love, and get married.

Excuses often heard are:
- I have to work overtime.
- I have to make sacrifices now.
- I have to travel a lot.
- I have to take work home.
- I am just too tired to make the effort.

Excuses will not get you what you want. The busier you are, the more important it is to meet someone. Then you won't have to waste time searching for the right mate or be distracted by constant thoughts of doing so.

Too Much to Offer

The more that you have going for yourself, the fewer people you will have to choose from who have your potential. This is not necessarily a disadvantage. Quantity is not always better. Nor does it mean that you have to lower your standards.

It is often assumed that you have more social options if you have less to offer. Whether you have more or less to offer than other single people, take action when you see someone interesting. Women who have become doctors or lawyers or have achieved high positions in the corporate world often believe that it will be nearly impossible to find a suitable mate. Sure, some insecure men will be frightened away, but some men would not be interested in you if you were the Queen of Sheba. More men will be interested if you present yourself in an approachable, unthreatening way. If you are looking for a house-husband who doesn't mind that your salary is larger than his, look for humanities-oriented men rather than fellow business people. If you have made yourself a success in the corporate world, there is no reason not to have success in your social life.

If you are the chief of surgery, this doesn't mean you cannot find a suitable husband. You may be limiting yourself too much if you worry about titles and societal propriety. The kind of mate you will be comfortable with will be able to see the big picture and fit into yours.

What Do You Do for a Living?

Professional or executive women must delicately answer men who ask what they do for a living. How you handle this question sets the stage for future advances. You must tell a man what you do without posing a threat. If you have a doctorate in physics and are a professor at a college, you might say, "I teach science at Rider College," and wait for the response. Listen and observe carefully. If the man seems really taken aback, or uncomfortable, casually switch the topic so he can get to know other things about you. Once he gets a sense of you, he may be a lot less concerned with your greater success—unless he is very insecure.

Are You a Female Businessman or a Woman in Business?

There are a limited number of eligible female executives. Most are married, have boyfriends, or are not available for one reason or another. Men's experiences with female executives are therefore limited. Many men believe that female executives are cold and calculating, less feminine than other women, and more difficult to deal with. The conservative executive dress code for women reinforces this concept. Lower- and middle-level male executives often feel threatened by an executive woman who has equal authority. When dating, therefore, an executive woman might want to consciously project her femininity to dispel any negative stereotypes.

Talking to the Professional Man

If you want to be more comfortable with a male executive, make sure you understand something about corporate life. One way to have a sense of involvement is to read *Business Week*, *The Wall Street Journal*, and

Fortune. A few books on the subject should give you an overall view. You could also attend some business seminars or lectures. Awareness will breed confidence even if you have had limited exposure to corporate life. Many executive men will perk up when they can converse intelligently with their dates about subjects that engage them so much at work.

What Professional Men Want

There are three types of male executives: those who prefer executive women, those who prefer nonexecutive women, and those who have no particular preference. Let's look at these three types and some possible reasons for their preferences:

Prefer executive women:
- They have things in common to talk about.
- They have the appropriate status.
- They enjoy friendly competition.
- They have had bad experiences with non-executive women.

Prefer Nonprofessional Women:
- They offer no competition.
- They help him get away from work.
- They tend to be more "traditional."
- They have had bad experiences with executive women.

No preference:
- They are open-minded and evaluate each woman on her merits.

- They have had positive experiences with both executive and nonexecutive women.

You Have Not Waited Too Long

If you have postponed your social life and marriage too long or have just awakened to realize that you are now thirty-four, successful, but lonely—it is not too late to incorporate a meaningful social life within your busy corporate career. You will need to sort out your objectives. To be a complete person you need both a personal and a professional life. It can be lonely at the top, but it doesn't have to be. It is not an either or situation. You may find that you have not paid enough attention to your personal life because it is harder to exert the same comfortable control as in a business situation.

Dating a Busy Professional

In order to date and have a good relationship with a successful executive, you have to understand how he or she thinks and acts. You will have to fit into a tight schedule, trying not to feel like a second-class citizen. Take solace in the fact that the powered man or woman executive wouldn't bother with you in the first place if he or she were not interested. Such busy people don't often have relationships where they constantly hold hands and stare into your eyes. Executives often sacrifice their personal lives to maintain their edge.

Just because an executive doesn't have much time to go looking for a mate doesn't mean that he or she will compromise and go out with just anyone. On the contrary, those few hours a week that the two of you are sharing might will represent one hundred percent of his or her social life. Consider it a compliment, then, that you monopolize the human side of that tycoon's life, and that you are in the number one position to pull off a lifetime merger with that person.

10

You Still
Have Time

"When you make
up your mind to get
married, you will be
astounded how fast
you will find the right
person to marry."

— Dr. Gallatin

189

Getting Started

Regardless of how long you have been single, whether you are legally separated with children, are divorced or widowed, you can find the right person to share your life with. The more you have going for yourself and the more people who know it, the sooner you will find the love you are seeking.

Dating no longer stops at twenty-one or thirty; many of us will be dating people at middle age and beyond. No one knows for sure when he or she will be dating again. Because being unmarried no longer inplies celibacy or "living in sin," we leave unloving and destructive marriages and relationships even if the world out there is uncertain and even foreboding. Since so many others have braved the trip back to the singles world, it now seems somewhat easier. A divorced parent with young children, however, finds this trek harder.

At least for a spell, many older singles opt for an alternative to marriage. They develop a long-term friend/lover relationship with someone who has the same feelings and life-style. They maintain separate apartments and friends while fostering a serious relationship. In effect, they are both "married" and single. Unless one or both of these "just good friends" have been seriously burned by the institution, such arrangements could slide into marriage.

In order to decide if marriage is for you, you have to look at what a good marriage will offer. You will have a regular sex life, someone who is concerned about you, and a steady companion. You won't have to deal with the problems of asking or getting asked out on dates.

It's Never Too Late to Say "Yes"

If you have not been married for many years or have been single, you may feel that marriage is not for you. You get increasingly hesitant to commit yourself and get accustomed to being single. You have to break this habit.

If you were formerly married, you must put it all behind you. Don't blame yourself or the institution of marriage. It may be that your marriage was more an emotional mistake or an economic decision than the product of well-balanced intentions.

Beware of the "Lonatic"

A lifelong unmarried person with few dates and relationships is harder to win over and change than an active single who hasn't yet found the right person. Singles who have never been married and have no sense of urgency often get so wrapped up in themselves that they become "married to themselves." The term I have coined to refer to these people is "lonatics." If you are not a lonatic and if you are serious about getting married, you are going to have to start doing things differently.

The longer you are single, the harder it will be to say "Yes." You first have to decide if you really desire to be married. If you do, then set yourself a deadline. Be convinced that you are on the way and that *you will be married in a year or less.*.

Getting Out There Right Now

Too often, people who haven't been married or are divorced or widowed don't feel any special need to begin seriously looking today or tomorrow—but "someday soon." The someday attitude won't work. "Someday" is not on the calendar. There is today and tomorrow. Think of today, not someday, if you want to be married.

Starting Over

I'M GOING OUT FOR A WHILE.
DON'T LET ANYONE IN UNLESS
HE'S TALL, DARK, HANDSOME,
ARTICULATE, AND AVAILABLE.

If you have been out there too long, you may be despairing, giving up even while you are going out. Just realize that you may not have been doing the best things all these years. You are holding this book right now, and right now is when you should begin doing things differently.

Divorced but Not Free

Once you have been married, even if only for a short time, it is often hard to be single again. Marriage is a good habit. Even if the marriage ended in a bitter divorce, good habits are the hardest to break.

Depending on your age or the situation, divorce can be very difficult to take and may require considerable readjustment. Today, with one of every two marriages ending in divorce, there are an awful lot of recycled singles who are determined to do it right the next time around.

All right, so you married the wrong person. You will be glad not to be married to that person, but not glad not to be married. The good times, those good days, months, and even years, have shown you how wonderful marriage can be. The sooner you start looking for a new mate the sooner you will be married.

On the Road Again

Regardless of who initiated the breakup, you need to pick up the pieces and get moving again. If he or she left you for another person, it will be more difficult to take than if your former lover or spouse just wants out of the marriage or relationship.

Instead of blaming yourself, see if you can correct any personal failings that may have come to light. Losing you will prove to be his or her loss. Adjust your new self in the mirror and get back on the road again. When you are on the road to a serious life partner, all roads lead to home.

Putting It Behind You

Whether your former spouse deserves it or not, you may fall into the trap of worshipping the memory of your relationship. Dwell on the areas where your new acquaintance is better than your former partner. Was your former husband or live-in girlfriend really a saint? If he or she was, look for a replacement who is just as good. It will just take a little longer.

It makes some difference if you were married for two years or for fifteen. If your marriage was for a short time, it was more an interruption in your singlehood than a changed state. In some cases, it is almost the same as if you were living together and broke up. You only got a taste of marriage.

It is one thing if you were married when you were deeply in love; it is another if you had serious second thoughts on your wedding day. A client named Barbara told me she sat across from her new husband and said to herself, "This is not going to be the man I will be with when I am sixty-five." A lot of marriages are more arrangements of convenience in one way or another than unions with one's dream partner. All marriages are hardly made in heaven, although some may feel that they were conceived there.

The Widow's Plight

Becoming a widow is a tragedy. Many widows never remarry or become emotionally involved with another man. This could mean fifteen or twenty years of being by yourself after many years of togetherness. The older you get, the less chance you have of remarrying.

The longer you were married and the more you were in love, the harder it will be to date others, get emotionally and sexually involved, and remarry.

The older widow feels that she has no choice but to accept reality. She is especially concerned about competition from younger women. After twenty or more years of marriage, how can she become involved with another man? A younger widow is much more able to find a new mate and continue her life. If you are widowed after five years of marriage, you should fight your disappointment and move on, unless you have serious problems.

You can find another mate as long as you are interested and still have your health. Mabel came up to me after a seminar on Long Island, New York, and told me that she was sixty-two, widowed for a year, and was dating again because she had no intention of spending the rest of her life by herself. What are your intentions? You may find that dating again will be less of an ordeal and more fun than you think. You just have to take the first step and do something today about improving your social situation.

Preparing Yourself for Reality

One way of adjusting to a change in marital status and to get valuable support and feedback is to join a group. Some groups are better than others. Visit a number of them and find one that suits your personality, needs and background. You will be able to share your thoughts with people who have had common experiences or to just sit back and observe.

Develop new friendships with like-minded people. The time between relationships or marriages can be constructively spent.

You should find out where your marriage failed, what you want in a mate, and the conditions that are necessary for you to get reinvolved. It may take a little

"Like Shirley MacLaine, Doris is fifty and has great legs."

while before you are emotionally involved again, but not forever. You want to discover the right person this time so you will never have to look again. Unfortunately, most people opt to be with the kind of person they are familiar with rather than the one who is best for them. Learn from your past behavior; find the best person for you.

The Good News

Many people think that love and passion are strangers to forty-year-olds. Yes, middle-aged people are no longer ruled by torrential hormones, but love and passion are things of the mind—and therefore they belong to all who think young. Pablo Picasso was a passionate lover well into his seventies.

Advantages of Being Over Forty

One way to increase your likelihood of finding a mate sooner is to appreciate the advantages of being over forty. The major benefits are:

You know more about yourself and others.
Living through the experiences of the good and the bad, you know more about yourself and others than ever before. Your judgment of character should be improved and should help to shorten the time it takes in deciding if someone is for you.

You have a clearer idea of what you want.
As we move through life, we are more aware of what we want and what we are willing to accept in a person. It is hoped that you are more realistic than young, moonstruck fools.

There should be less game playing.

Since you know the score by now, you can have more honesty in your relationships. You can be more direct and know quickly where you stand.

Your children, if any, will be older.

You can focus more of your attention on your relationship. Relax and enjoy yourself. Younger people have younger children at home, who present obstacles and create greater pressures.

Thirty-Nine Plus

Age is more of a concern for women and men with limited resources and education. Some women look better at forty than they did at thirty because they are more confident, dress better, are thinner, and have a hairdo that works. If at forty you are overweight, refuse to seriously make attempts to meet a mate, and wait for good fortune to strike, you will have a long, lonely time ahead of you.

Being forty-plus doesn't mean that you are forced to spend the rest of your life by yourself, even if you have never married.

If you were married for fifteen years, it may be more difficult because you are not accustomed to dating. If your last marriage was not so successful, draw on that experience to honestly define for yourself the characteristics you now believe your next mate must have for you to have a successful marriage. Then using the guidelines set forth in this book, spend the extra time and effort meeting people. Someplace out there, the one for you is waiting, guaranteed.

Dating Again

Reentering the dating arena at middle age is not exactly what you planned early on in life. You will want to look your best, have your weight fit your body, and dress to attract the appropriate attention. You will want to go to places that have less focus on the physical. If you are a woman, bars are a less desirable option once you are in your forties. If you don't look your age or are very self-confident, you could even be successful at a bar, but, generally speaking, your chances of success are greater where there are fewer younger women competing directly with you.

I recommend introductions and natural social opportunities in the course of your everyday life. The commercial singles scene has a limited number of activities for those past forty. This kind of forum is often not worthwhile as it attracts too many marginal people. Attend only the best of these activities. Refer to Chapter Two. Otherwise you are bound to be disappointed and will become unnecessarily discouraged.

Men will have a wider selection of choices because the right sixty-year-old can still interest a woman of forty-five. In addition, the higher the age group, the more lopsided the women-to-men ratio.

Middle Age Dating

When you are in your teens and early twenties, dating is fun in itself. It is part of the process of discovering yourself and is charged with sexual energy and excitement. As you grow older, dating becomes more of a job than fun.

In middle age, dating doesn't always have the sense of excitement that we might like it to have, at least from a man's point of view. Successful middle age dating occurs when a man adopts more of the woman's perspective. He has to mature, concerning himself with commitment and integrity rather than physical appearances.

Middle age dating is a much more refined art. The couple know how to go out, have more money to spend, and have more life experiences to share.

Exploding the Myths About Middle Age Dating

Myth	*Reality*
Dating should be the same at forty as it was when you were sixteen.	The manner in which we date has changed in many important ways. The new approaches are not all bad. Learn what you don't know and merge this with your personal realities.
Physical beauty is not that important.	Men like to be with and to be seen with women who look good. While you don't have to be a beauty queen, you do want to look your best and be as appealing as possible.

Experience and being older make you interesting and desirable.

Just because you have been around doesn't mean you are as interesting as you could be. You should still work at keeping up-to-date.

You're stuck if you are divorced or not married at middle age.

Maybe things have not worked out the way you designed them many years ago. It is never too late to turn your life around. Vow to do better and cut down on your mistakes. Once you find the right person, your age and past won't matter.

Others just like you are getting married, so don't give up and depend on good fortune.

A Younger Man!

If you are not attracting enough men in your age category, regardless of the reason, you can widen your options by going out with a somewhat younger man. He doesn't have to be your son's age. Some younger men would be interested in you. All healthy men are not looking solely for trim, bright-eyed younger women.

Comedian George Burns jokes, "I'd date women my own age, but there aren't any." Women live longer, George, and are increasingly hooking up with younger men. Today a woman can date and marry a younger man without any social stigma, as long as the age gap is not obviously too wide.

For you, going out with a man five years younger might make the difference between having a man in your life or not. A somewhat younger man with a little more energy may not be all that bad. Why date and marry an older man when you may be able to have a younger man? The important thing is to be with the right person for you, and not to let age dictate your life-style.

There is no reason why a younger man could not meet an older woman, find her desirable, and want to date and marry her. In fact, it happens everyday. I personally know a number of successful marriages along these lines.

Some younger men are more egalitarian, having fewer negative attitudes toward older women.

Why Women Don't Date Younger Men

There are four major reasons why older women don't date younger men:

- Fear of societal disapproval.
- Fear that others will think the man is looking for a "mother" figure.
- The misconception that younger men have less life experience and are not their equals.
- The fear that younger men are just using them temporarily.

These objections are no longer valid: sincere, healthy and lasting relationships with younger men have become increasingly common.

Winning Over a Confirmed Bachelor

Most women don't bother trying to win over a confirmed bachelor because his social skills may be limited and they feel that it will be a waste of time. With care, you can find a gem who has not been taken by some other woman. Since he may have had few deep relationships with loving women, he may appreciate you more than some other man who has had a seemingly endless string of relationships.

Married Too Many Times?

Today it is not uncommon to meet someone who has been married three or more times. Most people will not even give a person with this kind of track record a chance. While you may want to ask this person a lot of questions, you shouldn't automatically rule him or her out.

11

Dating For
Marriage

"Until you are
married, you are
just friends."
— Dr. Gallatin

205

Getting Started

After meeting someone good for you and beginning to date, you should turn the date into a relationship and let that evolve into a proposal of marriage. Dating is a game for some but not for you. You are seeking a marriage commitment. Dating should be viewed as a means to stop dating and to get married. If you follow the techniques outlined in this book, dating without the possibility of a lasting relationship can now be put behind you—no matter how many years you have been playing games.

When meeting a new potential mate, you must carefully evaluate that person. Is he or she your best possible choice? Here are some questions that you need to ask and answer. Putting your thoughts on paper will help.

WHY I Want a Relationship With _____
                                    (first name)

_____

_____

_____

_____

_____

_____

_____

Mistakes I Have Made in Previous Relationships That I Am Not Going to Repeat:

Mistake   **Remedy**

_____   _____

_____   _____

_____   _____

_____   _____

_____   _____

A typical relationship is not a commitment to marriage. No matter how close you are to someone, you are just very good friends until you are legally married. Too often relationships just seem to go on and on and on. Ask yourself what it is about your relationship or your present partner that is keeping you from tying the knot. If you are the one delaying marriage, perhaps you are suffering from a troubled past. You may want to seek professional help. It's possible that something about your parents' marriage is preventing you from going to City Hall.

Although looking for a marriage partner today is more complex than it has ever been, some things have not changed very much. For instance, the man is still the one who asks the woman out (with rare exceptions), he pays the bills (in most cases), picks up his date at her home or office, and chooses the restaurant or show.

Some rules of the game have changed, however, since the sexual revolution and the feminist movement. When a man dates a woman today, she is more apt to be pursuing a specific career. Her whole life will probably not revolve around her man. A woman's sexual behavior is also less predictable than in the past. Today's women are more likely to demand sexual compatibility, and the ratio of male to female heartbreakers has evened out a bit. With more female game-players out there, the dating game has gotten tougher for the marriage-minded man.

The result is that too many relationships are remaining fluid and not solidifying into commitments like marriage. If a steady date doesn't work out as a marriage partner, this person could end up becoming a friend. This "friend" often gets used as a transitional bridge, a confidant/lover kept hanging on until a better choice is found. The person you thought was embracing you was merely keeping you on hold. If you suspect that you are being used this way, force the issue and, if your suspicions turn out to be right, break off immediately. You might lose your friend and you may have to sleep alone, but if you want to be married in a year or less, you cannot be wasting time in dead-end relationships.

Dating Without Unnecessary Games

Dating is both fun and anxiety provoking, and often full of games—particularly at the beginning. Game playing prevents us from getting to know each other at the most critical times. The games begin the minute you say "hello," and with some people can go on indefinitely. In order to achieve a sincere rapport immediately, you want to create a climate of acceptance and involvement.

Most people play those games in the belief that they have to protect themselves from potential rejection. They don't want to show weakness or vulnerability. You may not be able to eliminate games, but you can minimize them considerably. The more straightforward you are, the more the other person will be comfortable in being natural.

AND THAT'S WHEN I DECIDED
THERE ARE WINNERS AND LOSERS
IN THIS WORLD AND I WAS GOING
TO BE A WINNER. SO I GOT MY RÉSUMÉ
TOGETHER AND BEGAN
MY SEARCH!

You should eliminate games at the start of a relationship because the first three dates are critical. When you don't play games, you more quickly discover what you want and need to know from a potential partner. You can be at ease and sincere with a little extra effort. Slowly open up about yourself and listen carefully as your date responds in kind.

Dating Should Be Fun

You may have had many fun dates since junior high school. The purpose of dating for marriage, however, is to discover if the person you have selected is good for you. Of course your dates should be enjoyable. After the third date, when you have made your decision to get involved with someone, the fun really begins.

Do's and Don'ts of the First Three Dates

Focus Your Energy on Getting to Know the Person.
You want to confirm your initial and subsequent impressions, both over the phone and in person.

Spend an Appropriate Amount of Money.
You don't have to break the bank. Excessive spending or not spending enough will make your date uncomfortable and will promote game playing. When someone else is paying at a restaurant, you cannot lose when you order something in the middle price range.

Pick Activities You Both Like.
It might be best to save the expensive glitter after you are both emotionally involved. Suggest activities but

defer to your partner's wishes as long as they are reasonable. The person is more apt to be attracted to you if you do things that he or she especially likes. Stick to your guns and decline that roller derby date, though you don't have to say that you find it repulsive.

Both Partners Should Be Involved in Decision-Making.

You get to know the person better and more quickly if you discuss things with him or her. See how the other party handles decisions. If you don't want to be the sheep or the shepherd in a relationship, establish parity right away.

Use Your Sense of Humor.

You will loosen up and learn more from your date by using your sense of humor. A conversation stacked with carefully calculated questions will only convince your partner that he or she is on trial.

Discover as Much as You Can About the Other Person.

Even if you have to supplement your dates and phone conversations with a little research, you want to find out as much as you can about your date. You must discover if this person meets your basic expectations and your "Ideal Marriage Partner" profile.

Be Cautious But Think Positively.

You must strike a balance. Looking only for negative things and forgetting the positive points about your date will make it harder for you to turn a quality dating partner into a loving spouse.

Watch for Key Nonverbal Signals.

Look for consistency between the verbal and non-verbal signals that you get, and note any trends. See the discussion on body language in Chapter Five.

Keep an Open Mind.

Go with the flow. Planning your every activity or predicting your emotional state is not possible.

Take Your Date Away From Home.

She is used to her stomping grounds. Make your meeting something special by shifting the scenery. He was full of confidence in the sports environment of your first date. Meet him in a cultural, religious, or business context to see if he is multidimensional.

Don't Discuss Past Relationships.

Your date is interested in you and doesn't want to know about your involvement with others. With the exception of general facts, such as one's marriage history, keep such information to a minimum.

Don't Wear Your Problems and Insecurities on Your Sleeve.

Someone who barely knows you is not interested in solving all your problems and self-doubts. Gain your date's admiration, rather than his or her sympathy. Besides, it's not fair to cheat on your therapist that way.

The First Three Dates

In most instances it will take you three dates and a number of phone calls spread over approximately three weeks to determine if someone special is more than a nice person and has what it takes to warrant your getting emotionally involved.

If you go out with someone especially complicated, it may take you a little longer before deciding. How much longer depends on your perceptiveness and your partner's. In most cases you should invest no more than two additional dates.

Don't budget yourself a couple of months with someone you can't figure out. It is important that you don't waste valuable time or energy with the wrong person. You want to be married within a year.

The First Call

Now that your skills have earned a phone number, the next step is making the call. Wait a day or two before placing the call. Let the person anticipate hearing from you.

The purpose of your call is to reconfirm your interest, to see if he or she is still interested, and to learn a little more about each other. You may not have had much time to chat and formulate an opinion, and, probably, neither of you was very open.

When you call, introduce yourself and remind the person where you met. Ask if he or she has a few minutes to chat. A first conversation over the phone with someone who is not relaxed is no way to get what you want and need to know.

Some people love to speak over the phone, whereas others prefer quick telephone conversations. And some will reveal more over the phone than others. In any case, try to keep this first conversation brief. No matter how comfortable both of you may be, it is better to leave some mystery and anticipation for your first date.

You don't have to initiate or accept a date if, after talking, you change your mind. If you are no longer inspired, end it now before wasting any more time. If you were too liberal about taking or giving out phone numbers, be more discriminating next time.

Closing the Call

When you decide that you have talked long enough, take the "Yes" or "No" plan of action:

A "Yes" Response

"It has been fun talking with you. I would like to get together for _____."

                (some activity you'll both enjoy)

Pause for the response and then continue:

"How about Friday at 7:30? (Set up a specific day and time and an alternate one; or let the other person provide an alternate.) Make sure you each have a number where you can be reached in case something comes up at the last minute.

A "No" Response

"Thanks for calling me" or "thanks for talking. I have to go now. Take care of yourself." Hang up immediately without making excuses.

Don't be flustered if you get an answering machine. Just say, "Hi _____ , this is _____ . We met last week at _____ and I just thought I would say hello. If you would like to get back to me, you can reach me at this number in the evening _____ . If you have a minute during the day, my work number is _____ . I hope to hear from you soon."

It is hard for some women to initiate a call after numbers are exchanged. You could always open by saying that you have been hard to get on the phone, and that you want to make sure he wasn't calling while you were out of town or while your phone was turned off. If he is interested, he should pick it up from here and ask you out. If he doesn't ask you out, then say, "It was nice talking with you, take care. . . " and hang up. You didn't get a good connection.

Before Your First Date

Be ready and be relaxed. Here are some tips to make your experience better:
- Anticipate having a good time, but don't expect the time of your life.
- Allow enough time so you don't have to meet your date while you are catching your breath and full of excuses for being late.
- Wear clothes that are appropriate and comfortable.
- Be as rested as possible so you will be alert.
- Carry enough money to get you home comfortably and to take care of any unanticipated expenses.

First Time Out

First dates make us apprehensive because they are akin to a job interview or an audition.

A first date is a cause for both excitement and anxiety. The purpose of getting together is to see if there is any potential for the two of you. The way to achieve your purpose is to have good judgment, genuine interaction, and a minimum of stress.

If you have been actively dating and having regular relationships, you probably won't make more out of a first date than you should. The more you expect from it, the more anxious and desperate you will appear and the less chance you will have of doing well.

If you are getting together with someone from a personal ad, a computer dating service, or a relative's recommendation you have to consider the date as strictly an exploratory get-together.

Be positive. Allow one to two hours for the first date together, meeting for a drink or for coffee and dessert.

Avoid trapping yourself for a long activity or in an exclusive restaurant. No matter how good the person initially looked, it is amazing how different your impression may be ten minutes after talking to him or her at a second meeting. Sometimes that first date is barely recognizable the second time around.

If on meeting a blind date you discover that this person has misled you, there is no point in wasting any more time or money. Simply and straightforwardly say, "There seems to be some misunderstanding. You represented yourself as being something that you are not. I am awfully sorry, but this is not going to work out. I am disappointed, but our getting together was contingent on what I was originally told. Take care of yourself." Turn around immediately, walk away at a normal pace, and forget you ever saw this person. Don't feel you are being rude if you don't suffer through a date that is not working out. The Lord hasn't called you to a life of martyrdom.

If you don't have the nerve to leave right away, you can sulk until the person gets the message. And then leave. Another way out is to say you have had a hectic day and you are a little pressed for time. Tell the person that you didn't want to cancel but that you only have about fifteen minutes. When the time is up say, "It was nice talking with you. I have to get going now. Take care."

What Do We Do?

A show may be very appealing, but chatting about the quality of the acting and the musical score is less helpful in determining the kind of person your date is. Plan to spend some time with few distractions, where it is easy to converse. You can get a lot of mileage out of a walk around the reservoir.

The type of date you have should depend on how you met and on how long you have known each other. If you have been talking after church for six months and have finally decided to go out, then a show or a fancy dinner is in order for the first date.

Two on the Town

Dating can eat up much money. Breaking the bank isn't necessarily the best way to get what you want or to win someone over. I know a man of limited means who would spend a hundred dollars on a first date. Women expect men to spend only what they can afford. Most women are more concerned with how men treat them and how they use the resources they have. If a woman is disappointed with an inexpensive date, this is a danger signal to the alert male of worse things to come.

Afterwards

At the end of your date you have to make one of three possible choices regarding the prospect of dating that person further:

You are interested.
You are not interested.
You are not sure.

If you are in category one or three you should initiate or consent to a second date.

It is very important to reflect carefully on each date before deciding to keep seeing the person.

We are often not sure about our feelings or assessments. If you have some doubts, give the person another shot. Even if it doesn't lead to a permanent relationship, you are not wasting your time. If you couldn't eliminate the person right off, he or she must have something to offer you.

You should both be more relaxed on the second date and be able to find out what you need to know. Have specific questions in mind so that you can bring them up at the appropriate time.

Between Dates

It is very important that you do some serious thinking between each date, especially between the first and second and the second and third. Reflect on what you have reservations about, not just what you like. Writing your thoughts down helps to focus your inner feelings. After each date, take out these notes and review them. Add to and subtract from your assessment. Before writing someone off too quickly, examine all your options.

Ending a Date Early

On occasion, you may decide that you made a mistake and want to call it a day as soon as reasonably possible. It is best to end a date on good terms. Many people are uncomfortable following this advice, so they cause a scene or treat their dates with disrespect once they lose interest.

The following approaches may leave your date disappointed, but not angry:

"_____ , I have to get up earlier tomorrow
    (Date's first name)
than I had planned and I will have to go home shortly.
I am sure that you can understand."

"_____ , my stomach has been upset all
    (Date's first name)
day, but I didn't want to cancel our date. I was hoping
that I'd be feeling better by now. I am going to have to
go home now because I really don't feel well. I am sure
that you can understand."

If your date asks you if you are mad and don't want
to see him or her again, respond by saying:

"The _____ was nice. Give me
        (activity; for example, dinner)
a call if you like, and we will see what we can do."

Be careful not to upset your date too much if you
need a ride home or if your safety or comfort could be
in jeopardy. Do not make a series of excuses. Keep your
remarks brief.

Date Two

The purpose of the second date is to confirm what
you have learned so far and to see if your interest is
sustained. On the second date you want to look for
undesirable traits that were not visible when the person
was most on guard. You have an opportunity to see the
person in a new setting. If the first date was at an art

museum, the second date could be a dinner where you would get to know a different side of the person.

A second date can be more like a first date if that was a brief meeting or if you went to a movie and had little interaction. The same thing is true if you or your date was quiet or cautious, or if you were on a double date where the dynamics are different.

It is still too early to decide on the nature of the relationship. A man doesn't yet know if he is liked or being used. A woman doesn't yet know if the man wants her, her body, or both. Neither of them knows if the dating partner's interest is temporary or long-term.

End It at Date Two if the Person Is Not for You

Sometimes we are very hesitant to stop after one date, even if we feel negative right off the bat. If you want to be married as soon as possible, you must cut your losses immediately. Getting comfortable with the wrong person is one of the major mistakes that singles make.

If you thought the person was for you and subsequently discover new information to the contrary, it is time to say good-bye in the best possible manner. After two dates it is easy. After six months it takes more effort.

Date Three

In most cases this is the critical date. During or after this date both parties decide whether a relationship is possible. If it is "Yes," it may be signaled by an escalation of physical contact and verbal intimacy.

Even if it takes a few more dates to decide, you and the other party should have most of the basic information you need to decide upon launching a bona fide relationship.

Dr. Gallatin's Eight Steps to Know if Someone is a Serious Possibility

A relationship that lasts for months is a failed one. Only if it leads to years of commitment, preferably marriage, can you call a relationship a success. It is not the quantity but the quality of the dates you get that counts.

It is my contention that you only need four weeks to gauge one's personality and basic values, and to know if he or she is a serious candidate for marriage. You will get results if you follow the eight steps.

Step One

You went to a party Friday night, spoke for fifteen minutes to someone whom you got good vibes from, and exchanged home numbers.

Step Two

Call between two and four days later, talk between fifteen minutes to half an hour. If still interested, ask out or accept a date from this person.

Step Three

Go out on a Friday night or Sunday afternoon when both the workweek and the weekend offer the fewest pressures. Meet for a drink or a leisurely walk. Share a meal if the chemistry is good, but nothing expensive this soon.

Step Four

Call two days later and talk between a half hour and forty-five minutes. Set up another date.

Step Five

Go out either Friday, Saturday, or Sunday.

Step Six

Call to talk for a half hour or so, and set up a date for Saturday.

Step Seven

Go out on a date.

Step Eight

Call and chat as long as you like. Decide now, if you haven't after the last date, whether it is "go" or "no go."

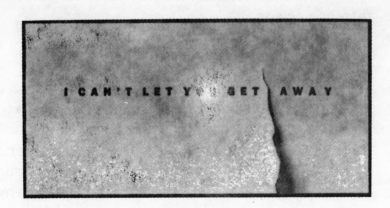

Benefits of the Eight Steps

In one month you will have had opportunities to determine if this person is for you.

You will have seen the person in a number of different settings and moods.

You will have invested a minimum of time, money, and emotion.

Dating More Than One Person at a Time

It is not wise to date one person exclusively, unless you have decided that this is the person with whom you want to get emotionally involved. The key to successful dating is balancing your emotional energy and your time. Seeing two people improves your odds of landing a solid marriage prospect, and gives you the perspective of comparison.

You won't clutter up your social life if you follow the policy of deciding within three dates whether to continue going out or not. You will also avoid the problems and hazards of becoming sexually involved with more than one person.

Building a Lasting Relationship

Relationships work best when both people have a lot in common and see the world the same way. Up to this point it was all right to know your date's favorite music, sport, or meal. By now you should know how your new friend expresses affection or thinks about major issues. You want to go beyond the whats to find out the whys.

You must accept certain problems or decide how you are going to deal with them. You also have to decide on what kind of timetable your relationship will run before reaching goals like engagement and marriage. Such decisions will be based on your expectations, personalities, and circumstances.

You want to develop a solid lifetime relationship even if you have limited social experience. Good relationships are a result of effort, commitment, compromise, and risk. If your record of social success is not what it could be, you might consider some type of counseling.

The past is over for both of you. A new couple is a new entity.

Dr. Gallatin's Pointers for Developing a Lifetime Relationship

- Focus an appropriate amount of energy on your partner.
- Don't be possessive.
- Expect occasional differences.
- Be considerate.
- Find out what things are important to your partner.
- Tell your partner what you want.
- Accept the person for what he or she is. Only assume that you will influence your partner's behavior a little at a time.
- See the person as an equal rather than a savior, parent, or child figure.
- Don't expect your partner to be able to satisfy your every requirement. Concentrate on the most important ones.

How to Get Over a Plateau

After you have been going out with someone a while, you tend to reach a plateau. Those relationships that have more depth take longer to reach this point of leveling off. Don't expect the earth to move. If the earth moved last month and doesn't this month, it doesn't mean you cannot sustain a good and permanent relationship.

At the beginning, relationships are exciting because you don't know the person very well. As you get more familiar, you get into a routine. If you still love the person, but are tired of the routine, suggest new activities and scenery.

Types of Intimacy

Not everyone is looking for the same degree of intimacy. The amount of intimacy you desire will determine the kind of relationship you will be most happy in. Find someone with a compatible level of intimacy.

Continuous intimacy: Requiring constant touching and affection.

Normal intimacy: Enjoying physical contact, including hand holding in public when appropriate.

Low intimacy: Desiring little physical contact, with no body contact in public.

Allow for cultural and personality differences before condemning your partner as a possessive exhibitionist or a cold fish.

Getting Serious

By the end of the third month you should know each other well enough to decide on a tentative commitment to each other. The actual time depends on the couple's maturity, age, and experience, and on the quality of their relationship. If both of you are twenty-one, more than three months may be needed. If you have seen your partner in a variety of circumstances and have something strong and sure, you should get formally engaged by five or six months.

Commitment comes in a series of stages, each with an appropriate level of involvement. For example, you start going out once a week and then begin seeing each other twice a week. Within two or three months you both decide to see each other exclusively. You then spend more time with each other, maintain daily contact, and organize more of your life around each other's desires and obligations. Successful relationships come from doing things in a progressive manner, keeping sight of both the good aspects and the potential problems of each step. At each step you assess the situation and see if it is still "go."

All of this careful development is sacrificed, of course, when you sublet your apartment and move into your lover's place during the first several weeks of a relationship.

Reaching a Commitment

Commitment means that you have stopped looking elsewhere. You accept the person who is close enough to your ideal mate. You desire to build together and work things out with genuine love and concern.

Allergic to Marriage

Falling in love with someone who will not or cannot marry you is what you need to avoid. By the third date you should have ascertained the other person's opinions on marriage and children. Investigate a longtime unmarried person and one who has broken an engagement. Make sure that the person is not allergic to marriage, even if he or she likes the idea of being engaged. There are too many little boys and girls out there who are only too happy to have you move in and play house. These thirty- and forty-year-old kids have made silent marriage vows—vowing never to get married.

A woman in my Minneapolis *How To Get Married in a Year or Less* seminar complained about her thirteen-year live-in relationship. Marriage was never verbally ruled out, but the couple may not make it to a church before their funeral.

Right on Schedule

If everything is going along well, you should commit yourself to getting married by the fifth month. But before getting that marriage license, many couples may want to get a learner's permit.

Living Together

An article in *U.S. News and World Report* stated that more than two million unmarried couples are living together. Whether one should live with a future spouse is both a moral and a practical question. Here we will concern ourselves with the practical.

Whether for a trial marriage, convenience, or economics, living together has become common and acceptable for many people. Such "trial marriages" have not made a dent in the divorce rate and are not reliable indicators of permanent compatibility.

Many couples see living together as a logical step toward the eventual goal of marriage, and a means of finalizing their commitment. Those people who support living together before marriage say that having many dates or spending weekends or vacations together is not the same as living with someone day in and day out.

Dr. Gallatin's Guidelines for Living Together

- Set a specific deadline to get married. If you move on December 1st, agree to set a wedding date by March and to hold the ceremony in June.
- Keep your current residence. This way you can leave at any time for any reason.
- Don't publicize your living arrangements and needlessly alienate people who that don't agree with your life-style.
- Share your host's expenses but not the rent; don't let economics be a factor in your lover's assessment of your worth.
- Keep your friends and stay involved with them.

Have a State of the Union Meeting

You want to establish direct and honest communication from the beginning. To maximize the chances of success, I recommend having a "state of the union" dinner on the anniversary of your first date every other month. If you met on June 15, your first state of the union meeting would be August 15. If you have gotten this far, then it is worth realizing your potential.

It is suggested that you get together at a dinner in a romantic setting. An anniversary makes the occasion special and sentimental. Tell her that you want to celebrate your second month together in a special way. How can she turn you down? Bring her flowers. Don't announce your intentions in advance.

Once you have been seeing each other for two months or more and have gotten somewhat involved, neither of you should object to committing your thoughts to a few minutes of candid discussion.

If you are both excellent communicators who express your feelings easily, you won't need a formal "state of the union." Periodically focusing your feelings and intentions in this way could prove valuable nonetheless.

If you are the type who is hesitant to bring up certain subjects, these dinners will provide a mutually agreeable opportunity for expression.

On these occasions you will be able to air differences, set ground rules, check agreements, and reaffirm your caring. Evaluate where your relationship is going and where you'd like it to go.

Do You Need a Private Eye?

Private investigators are now soliciting business from singles by promising to check the background of anyone you are seeing or considering for marriage. One service asks the question, "Is he or she everything they claim to be?"

Before you get married, it is wise to sit down with your fiancee and get all your serious questions answered. If you are considering marrying someone who has been married a number of times or has had a complex background, it might not be a bad idea to check his credit or to inquire about her family.

Prenuptial Agreements

Mention drawing up a prenuptial agreement, and many people take a step backward. Not everyone needs one. If you are young and just starting out, it serves little purpose. If you have considerable assets, on the other hand, a prenuptial agreement will make sure the person is marrying you for youself.

Prenuptial contracts are becoming increasingly popular because more people have been married more than once and at all stages of life. These agreements are legal in an increasing number of states.

An agreement that stipulates who will do the dishes and laundry may be going too far.

How to Get Him to the Altar

- ❦ Shower him with attention (and occasionally in the shower).

- ❦ Be a little mysterious.

- ❦ Show him you know your way around the kitchen.

- ❦ Make yourself as attractive as possible (don't hide your best parts).

- ❦ Don't hide your brains.

- ❦ Be charming but secure in your self-worth.

- ❦ Follow his leads with any public displays of affection.

- ❦ Dress appropriately (the park is not the opera house).

- ❦ Be comfortable with yourself.

- ❦ Be a good lover (keep headaches to a minimum).

How to Get Her to the Altar

❦ Shower her with attention (even during the playoffs).

❦ Regularly let her know how much you love her, both verbally and non-verbally.

❦ Shed a few tears (if she's the emotional type).

❦ Display a great sense of humor (but don't be a stand-up comedian).

❦ Dress well (even when you feel like your favorite torn jeans).

❦ Be an unselfish lover (ask her what she wants).

❦ Be financially responsible.

❦ Be comfortable with yourself.

❦ Listen more and talk less.

❦ Be trustworthy and punctual.

12

❧

Single Parents:
New Loves And
Families

"Someone good is
looking for you."
— Dr. Gallatin

235

Make Time For Love

J ust because you are single and a parent doesn't mean you have to be lonely or have a date once in a blue moon. While your social life may not be quite as active as when you were a "swinging single," it can be better balanced and more rewarding. In *Sex & The Single Mother*, author Dawn B. Sove points out that "there are over six million divorced, widowed, and never-married mothers." You're not home alone. When we are used to being married it's difficult not to be in a loving relationship, sharing life's joys and travails with someone who cares.

Being a single parent seeking a spouse is not easy. You may have to pick a certain night to go out, juggle your work schedule, engage a baby sitter, and be home at a particular time. You may only have three hours that one evening a week in which to go out. Time is precious. It is tempting to put off going out when you have your hands full managing a busy household—but don't.

Whether you have been married once or three times you can still be swept off your feet by the person of your dreams. If you are only 28 and have two young children, there is no reason to spend your life by yourself or have an affair with a safe, married man. Even if you are a middle aged widow and your marriage was everything you wanted, you can surprise yourself by falling in love again. When you seek and find the right person you will quickly heal from previous relationships and put everything in its proper perspective.

Children aren't a substitute for marriage. Many single parents I have counseled mistakenly believe that if they have small children they cannot have a love life until their children are older or out of the house. Take that abundant concern for the children and be determined to get them a new daddy or mommy.

A Year Is Enough

Single parents have the same opportunity to be married in a year as those without children. Having children does mean you have to be determined, disciplined and a good manager of your life. While it may take you longer than you would like to meet a partner, once you do things should move right along nicely. You will actually have an easier time eliminating the game players, since your children will scare away anyone not ready for marriage or parenthood.

Not Again

If your marriage ended in divorce you may be held back by the fear that your next marriage could end up the same way. If you were young and innocent then, you now have another chance. This time you are wiser and know better what type of person will make you happy.

Even if you did make a mistake the last time, it's not a direct reflection of your self-worth, current abilities or state of mind. You just made a mistake. Now you would make a different decision.

You don't have to marry the same type of person again just because others seem to. Date the type of person who is good for you and you will end up happily married forever.

Digging Up Bones

It will be more difficult to find a new mate if you have not put your past to rest, especially if you got a raw deal. Regardless of the reason why you are divorced or widowed, tell yourself that you and your life are now different. While the past is not merely history, in time your reinterpretations of past events will make it all feel better. Walking around full of anger, shame and resentment will not get you married. Even if you are not completely recovered, it's time to get on with your love life. The distractions of a new romantic interest do wonders for the healing process.

When you start venturing out and dating you may not be at your best. You will have flashbacks of your spouse when a man you hardly know attempts to hold your hand or kiss you—even if you want him to. These flashbacks are normal and will diminish in time. You are charting new territory with someone you don't know well and will be a little hesitant. This is natural. You may have to push yourself to get out. When you begin to meet prospective spouses you will feel like your old self. Let bygones be bygones.

Single and a Mother

Families headed by single mothers now make up eight percent of all households. It is easier and more socially acceptable to raise children by yourself today. Holding down a job, running a family *and* looking for a new husband can be daunting. Make up your mind you are going to find a husband and manage everything else without driving yourself crazy.

Have a powwow with your children. Explain to them that you will be going out hopefully to find a husband. Reassure them that they have only one father who cannot be replaced. Tell them you will be dating a number of men until you find one that is special. When you do meet someone you really like you will be sure to introduce him. Reassure them that you love them. Don't be secretive about what you do on your dates, but they don't have to know everything. Handled properly, everything will work out great.

Single Dads

Single dads are very available for dating. One study showed that half of these fathers were dating at least once a week, and another twenty percent were going out once or twice a month.

There are two types of single dads: those that are raising their children and those who aren't. Men who raise children by themselves are rare, but you might run into one, and one is all you need. Only one and one-half percent of all households are headed by single dads. A father who is willing to raise his children is very desirable because he is responsible and caring. A single father won't mind if you have children, since he's used to the usual problems of raising children. Single dads are more apt to pitch in with the housework.

Single dads raising a family will be quite understanding of a single mother's situation. He may have a nagging ex-wife, legal problems and older children with tuition burdens, but he can be a great husband and a very good step-parent.

Too Busy for Love

We find time for what we want. If a single mother was offered a two week fully paid vacation in Rio with no strings attached, I bet she would quickly find the time to take the trip. No matter how busy you are, you have to make time to go to the supermarket. The next time you see someone who appears to be interesting and available at the deli counter line or at the baked goods section, why not open a conversation by saying, "These muffins sure look yummy. Have you tried them?" Even if the other person hasn't, he could say, "No, as a matter of fact I haven't. This week I am sticking to fruit." All you have to say is "why?" Your conversation has taken off. You might be surprised how long the conversation will last and how much you will enjoy it. Your respective shopping carts will offer many opportunities to slip in something about *his* groceries. You might decide to have a cup of coffee together and exchange phone numbers.

Back in Circulation

When you have been out of circulation for a number of years, you usually have to force yourself to go out and meet potential mates. If you don't know any other single parents, start meeting some. They will encourage you to venture out, perhaps even on a double date. You don't have to date the first man who asks you out. Once you start going out you will look forward to it. You will have new hope that you could find a new partner, be married and move on with your life.

Dr. Gallatin's Seven Tips for Single Parents

It isn't easy for a single parent to find a mate and you may become discouraged. At times you may feel nothing will ever happen. But someone out there is waiting for you. You will be on your way to getting married if you follow the seven tips below.

Tip No. 1
Make Up Your Mind to Find a Mate

In order to do what is necessary to meet a mate you have to really want to find someone special. This doesn't have to become an all-consuming obsession—just a major priority. You are not desperate, just rather desirous. Looking the slightest bit desperate will only reduce your chances of finding the best possible partner.

If you listen to some of your friends you could soon believe that you'd better grab any man you can before it is too late. You have more options than you may think, but you will have to take advantage of every opportunity. You won't have to settle for a lot less than you want, but you are more realistic than you were years ago.

Tip No. 2
Forget the Statistics

In *Beating The Marriage Odds* author Dr. Barbara Lovenheim cites a study at the University of Wisconsin. It points out that "One quarter of the women with one or two children don't remarry; two fifths of the women

with three children or more don't rewed." This report
shows that the more children a woman has, the less
likely she will remarry. The fact that most don't marry
doesn't mean that you cannot marry. Statistical correla-
tions and studies do not reveal intent. Forget the statistics and the probabilities! You only need one good one,
and that person is near you right now. The statistics are
only against you, if you let possibilities get away. Sure,
somebody always nabs the good ones. Let that somebody be you.

Even if you are a single woman over forty and have
less men available in your age category, there is no
reason why you couldn't find a mate. A man a few years
younger or older may be just what the doctor ordered.

Tip No. 3
Don't Let Your Children
Control Your Social Life

If you have young children, you might be consciously or subconsciously waiting for them to grow up
and leave the house. That is much too long a wait. You
love your children and might feel guilty for replacing
their father, but you know better than they do what is
good for you. You are not going to abandon your
children or yourself. When you are happy with your
social life you will be a better parent.

Children require time, money and energy. The more
children you have the more complex things become.
Children have a way of making it difficult for parents to
date by acting up just before you go out or by being rude
to your date. One woman's eight-year old son started

screaming whenever her date came to the door. A man with his own children will understand that your son is feeling threatened by this competition. Sit your son down a few minutes before your date arrives and explain to him that you love him and that this is your turn to go out on a "play date." Give him a big kiss and tell him when you will be back. There is no reason to feel any guilt. (A token gift from your date to your son could go a long way.)

Tip No. 4
Find Another Single Parent
to Be a Teammate

It will be a lot easier to get along if you have someone in a similar situation on your side. You can watch each other's children, support each other, go places together and not feel left out.

Tip No. 5
Be Sure Your Dating Skills
Are Current

Some things have changed since you were last out dating. Like anything else, your social skills can get rusty. When you haven't had a date in some time you will probably have some butterflies in your stomach. Ronald E. Wilson recalled his experience this way: "I had chosen the restaurant carefully, a charming country inn with a homey, intimate and romantic atmosphere. That evening, to my surprise, I found myself a little nervous. After all, why should I—a man with three grown children, sensible, experienced in the ways of the world widower—feel like an adolescent on a first date? I wondered if the conversation would drag. Would I say something foolish? Spill soup on my tie?"

The more you go out, the more comfortable you will feel and the better you will do. Soon you will be back in the swing of things. See Chapter Four, "Meeting. . . Wherever You Are" for a detailed review of current dating etiquette and tips.

Tip No. 6
Use Singles Activities
and Services Wisely

Dating services are especially popular with single mothers. Matchmakers can quietly screen candidates by using the specific requirements supplied, saving time, money and anxiety while keeping the whole thing discreet. It also minimizes the worst types of rejection.

Personal ads are another practical way for single mothers to screen candidates. You can answer ads that say "Children OK" or you can place an ad listing your minimum requirements. After talking with someone over the phone in the comfort of your own home you can meet for coffee after work or even have lunch. This is one way you can meet as many people as you like without hiring a baby sitter or introducing them to your children.

Single parents pressed for time find attending advertised singles activities very appealing. There is a single parents dating service in major cities to help you, and it's free. See Chapter Two "Going Out" for a complete review of singles services.

Tip No. 7
Don't Let Setbacks Stop You

Finding a new partner can at times be exasperating. Don't let a particular setback stop you. The more optimistic and determined you are, the sooner you will be married. If you are in a relationship that seemed made in heaven but didn't work out you should thank God for the unanswered prayer. The sooner you break up a no-progress or counter-productive relationship the better off you'll be. Unlike unencumbered singles, you can't clutter your limited social activities with secondary relationships that won't lead to a happy marriage.

Memory of Various Women

Drawing by W. Steig; © 1977 The New Yorker Magazine, Inc.

You Have No Competition

You may be wondering how you will be able to compete with younger women or more successful men or those who have less children. Just because someone has never married and has no children doesn't make that person more desirable. The older, never-married single can be less desirable, being pegged for someone unable to have a loving relationship. The blonde bombshell may be more shell than bomb.

As single parents you seem to be at an initial disadvantage, but your charm, sense of humor and conversation skills can make up for your complex resume. Your competitors have their own set of personal problems. You have no competition to be concerned about when you confidently present yourself well.

Your Love Choices

There are four kinds of prospective spouses to choose from. Divorced parents who are ready to settle down are at the top of the list. A divorced man who has grown children may enjoy being married to someone with younger children. Widows and widowers with children also make excellent possibilities, and, sadly, there are a surprising number of them in their 20's, 30's and 40's. Those who are legally separated are more distant possibilities. You will have to deal with their ongoing problems, and they are not available for marriage in the immediate future. If you will consider someone who has never been married you will have many more choices. Just because someone hasn't married and is not a parent doesn't mean that it cannot work out. He may enjoy having a ready-made family and be a terrific provider and parent. If you don't want to have any more children then a man who has not had a family may not be a good idea. He may tell you that he doesn't want to have any children but change his mind once he is married. Lastly, and most obviously, you cannot marry someone who is married. "I'll marry you as soon as I divorce Sally" is up there with "The check is in the mail."

Squeezing Sex In

If you have decided to have sex with the man you are dating, you are going to have to figure out how to keep it romantic, comfortable and regular. You may not be relaxed in a hotel even with a bucket of Champagne next to you. It's harder to have spontaneous sex when you have to get home to make dinner or attend a PTA meeting. How you handle the sexual side depends on many factors, including your attitude and your relationship with your children. If you have young children it's easier than having curious teenagers lurking around. After your children get to know your boyfriend he can actively take part in your family life. At this point it's easier to have him sleep over, ostensibly in a separate room.

Never Married, but a Parent

If you are a parent and have never been married, you too can be married in a year or less. The people you wouldn't accept will not accept you. The more open types that don't hold your background against you will be the ones willing to get serious in the first place.

There really is no difference in the way you go about meeting men. Your attitude and actions are the key to success. Don't let the fact that you have a child without a marriage certificate hold you back from going out and being socially involved. Self-consciousness could be your only obstacle.

You might want to wait a date or two before telling him about your child. This way you can give someone you like a chance to know and like you without the complications. It might help you to remember that he may have a complex background himself. If you have picked the right guy everything will be OK.

Not Your Children

When your date's children first meet you they will be indifferent or resentful. They will see you as an intruder. If you act friendly and accepting even when they act up you will pass their "test." Maintain control and you'll garner more respect and less resentment. Never act like they are in your way. While you aren't their parent, you can become good friends. Hopefully, you will like them, or at least get along. As the relationship grows the children can become more directly involved in outings. Show affection in physical ways only when you have allowed plenty of time to be accepted.

Congratulations

**"Here Comes
The Bride..."**

On Your Way

If you are using the ideas and techniques in *How To Get Married in a Year or Less*, you are on your way to getting married. You now know what to do. The rest is up to you. Some readers will have to make greater efforts than others.

Despite your best efforts, not everything will automatically go your way. Just keep plugging away and remember: you only need one good one, and that person is near you right now.

The ideas presented in this book have changed the lives of those people who have properly used them. Now that you have the inside track you know what to do and should be having fun doing it.

There have never been more singles. On the other hand, singles are left on their own as the family, the church, and neighborhood institutions provide few leads. When you correctly use what you have learned in this book you are not on your own. Romance, love and genuine caring should flow into your life like never before. When you do seem to be stuck or experience a serious setback, go to the appropriate chapters and sections to see how you can best handle the situation.

Invite Me To Your Wedding

You now know how to meet your marriage partner wherever you are, whenever you feel like it, in the most natural way possible without changing your personality, moving or getting a new job. In order to get the results you want, you need to put what you know in practice. Don't let other people's opinions or life's problems slow you down. Knowing what to do is not doing it. I look forward to be invited to your wedding.

"And the man on her right is
Dr. Martin Gallatin"

Hear Dr. Gallatin on Audio Tape

Now you can listen to Dr. Gallatin's inspiring programs while driving, walking, running, or sitting in your easy chair. Each tape is packed with practical advice that you can put to use immediately. Play these quality audio tapes whenever you feel like it.

Special One Hour Version
How To Get Married In a Year or Less
$6.95 Postpaid
$7.95 value

Titles	No.
How to Get Married in a Year or Less	100
Dating Without Games	101
Picking the Right Partner for Romance, Love, or Marriage	102

All tapes are 60 minutes
Entertaining • Uplifting • Practical Programs

All tapes $7.95 postpaid. New York residents add appropriate sales tax. Send your check or money order to:

Dr. Martin V. Gallatin
80 East 11th St., Suite 440
New York, NY 10003
(212) 228-2960

Call or write for complete list of tapes
and other products available.

FREE TAPE OFFER

SEND FOR YOUR FREE
30 MINUTE AUDIO TAPE TODAY

YES, Dr. Gallatin I want you to send me a FREE copy of your 30 minute audio tape *Making How to Get Married in a Year or Less Work* today.

I understand that the tape is absolutely FREE. I am enclosing $2.50 to cover postage, handling and insurance to ensure timely delivery.

Please print your name and address including zip carefully to ensure delivery.

Please feel free to photocopy this page.

Name _____

Address _____

City _____ State _____ Zip _____

Make check or money order payable to Dr. Gallatin.

Mail coupon to
Dr. Gallatin, 80 East 11th Street, Ste. 440, New York, NY 10003